from PAIN to PEACE

from PAIN to PEACE

HOW LIFE'S DIFFICULTIES CAN TEACH US PEACE

RICK BECHARD

ISBN: 978-0-692-23739-7

Author website: *rickbechard.com*

Typesetting by *www.wordzworth.com*

Published by Lucid Press, an imprint of Lucid Productions
www.lucidpro.net

Dedicated to my sister Linda.

Contents

Preface

There are moments in our lives that are crystal clear in our memories. We close our eyes and are transported back to that time. For me, one moment occurred when I was eleven years old. I was sitting in our kitchen in 1967 as my older sister, Linda, colored our mother's hair.

Linda has been a sage since she was young, carrying a philosophical and spiritual wisdom and desire to query everything. She suddenly broke the silence of the kitchen and said, "Just think: one day, all of us will be dead." As an eleven-year-old boy, I'm fairly sure that I had not yet considered my demise, and I wasn't pleased to have Linda propel me into its consideration.

My first concern was not one of my own mortality, but rather a deep, unimaginable fear that my mother would one day leave me. In the eleven years since she had given birth to me, she symbolized what love *must* be. There was no question in my mind that she would do anything for me; she never judged me, and always cared for and protected me. Whenever I was sick, I could see the concern on her face, and that alone was medicinal for me. I always felt safe in her presence.

Therefore, I could not fathom that my mother, who represented love in all its forms, could and would leave me. What would I do when she was gone? How could I feel safe? How could I go on? I wanted to understand these feelings, and I was already beginning to experience the pain of that unimaginable future loss. I had to get my mind around the idea of my mother's death, but at that young age, I had not yet acquired the tools necessary to help me deal with my fear.

This was certainly not my first worry as a child. I no doubt had frustrations about missing the local fair or not getting the grades I wanted, but this new anxiety, this new fear of losing my mother, had a depth with which I was unfamiliar. It was new territory and served as the impetus for me to examine what I was feeling for the first time in my life. I didn't learn much from that brief self-examination, other than the knowledge that I was really scared and sad about something that had no current reality.

Nonetheless, the experience stuck with me, and although my life continued after that night in the kitchen, it was never the same. From then on, I began to pay attention to all my thoughts and feelings. The concepts of life, meaning, and purpose permeated much of my world, and I frequently discussed what it all meant with Linda. Little did I know that my life's challenges would provide answers to the questions that haunted me. My trials and tribulations have taught me that we are *all* part of a perfect divinity, inherently whole and safe.

In a world filled with pain, guilt, judgment, and attack, the concept that we are as God intended can be hard to grasp, and my intention is not to prove this. Rather, this book is merely my attempt to explain why I have come to such a conclusion, and how this conclusion has resulted in a sense of inner peace, despite life's enduring challenges. This is my story. I have no need to attempt to change people and I am certainly not trying to preach. I hope you will view this book as an open discussion, and that you'll pretend that I'm your friend, sitting at a coffee shop, speaking to you about my life. So, let's enjoy our coffee together and perhaps you will discover that my life isn't so very different from yours.

ONE

A Fall from the Bed

"Sooner or later we all discover that the important moments in life are not the advertised ones, not the birthdays, the graduations, the weddings, not the great goals achieved. The real milestones are less prepossessing. They come to the door of memory unannounced, stray dogs that amble in, sniff around a bit and almost never leave. Our lives are measured by these."

—SUSAN B. ANTHONY

My entrance onto life's stage occurred in 1956. I played the role of a young boy on a rural farm in upstate New York. My supporting actors included my parents, four older brothers, and three older sisters. To this day, I'm still occasionally referred to as "the baby."

My earliest memory is from when I was four years old. It was nighttime. My bed was located in my parent's bedroom, and I remember crawling out of it, falling onto the floor, and striking my temple on something made of metal. The pain and my childish cries wakened me into human consciousness for the first time. The commotion woke my parents and I recall feeling safe as my mother picked me up and rushed me to the bathroom, with my father just behind her.

My mother placed a cold, wet washcloth on my injury and as I looked in the mirror, I made the firm connection that the reflection was my own. My wound was dressed and I remember how good it felt to have such attention and concern showered on me. Their love was more healing than the bandages. I slept between my parents for the remainder of the night, since my bed apparently contained unforeseen hazards.

Aside from the physical scar I received, that night was special because it introduced me to three things that would influence how I approached the rest of my life: the experience of fear, love, and the recognition of self. These were only vague impressions at first, yet I knew that they would have to be reckoned with in time. With this youthful insight under my belt, I continued to reach other conclusions about life. I understood that I was a boy and that wasn't going to change, and I believed that if I could experience fear and love at such an early age, they would most likely return.

I imagine that fear and love were present even as I was a newly arrived baby, but they were too abstract for my young mind to grasp. It took a fall from my bed as a slightly older child to help me comprehend fear and love, and it was the fear part that I knew I wanted to avoid in the future.

As my life continued, my sense of identity became even more specific. I lived on a farm and was part of a poor but proud and close family. One of my brothers, just two years older than me, was an angry child. For all my childhood and teenage years, I seemed to be the primary scapegoat for his anger. In his mind, I was one of the main causes of his unhappiness. I didn't understand his problems and I used to think he was upset because I took over his special role as the baby of the family. I noticed that my parents gave him more leeway, which seemed unfair to me, and their assurances that I would be "ahead in the long-run" were not satisfying. But as I look back, I understand what they meant. Clearly, they knew something I didn't.

In truth, all my siblings are wonderful, including my angry brother. I know any one of them would risk their life for me if they had to, and even though I relate to each of them differently, I love them equally. Like any family, some members simply connect on a level that is hard to define, and for me, I had such a relationship bond with Linda, the fifth child and middle girl.

It is hard to explain why we have deeper connections with some people and not others, but whatever the reason, Linda and I shared a special bond. I always got the sense that she saw things in me that I could not see in myself. For example, even though I had made a childhood commitment to avoid fear, I was afraid of almost everything and Linda knew this. Once, I was angry and crying about something, rocking back and forth and relishing my tantrum on the rocking chair in our living room. Linda came into the room and saw me crying, so she made funny faces at me. I fought her attempt to cheer me up for as long as I could, but laughter got the best of me. I remember how odd it seemed to be laughing and aggravated at the same time. I was intrigued that Linda had been able to take my tantrum away from me when I wanted to hold on to it for a bit longer. My feelings confounded me. How could I go from tears to laughter in less than twenty seconds? That day, I learned that my emotions could be fluid.

That memory reminds me of the funeral scene in *Steel Magnolias*. Sally Field's anger over the loss of her daughter appeared beyond control, and as a solution, Olympia Dukakis suggested that she slap her friend, played by Shirley MacLaine. There was a pause of uncertainty as everyone looked to see Field's reaction to such an incredible suggestion, and suddenly, they all burst into laughter. Like Dukakis, Linda turned my tears to laughter in a matter of seconds, and when she did, I learned that emotions could be variable. Even as a child, I knew this was a human phenomenon that I wanted to better understand, and I wondered if I ever would.

Not long after, in September 1961, my oldest sister, Diane, brought me to school for the first time. I remember taking the bus with Diane and her best friend, Louise, feeling excited and special as she showed off her little brother to her high school friends. This was going to be a good day, I thought, but I was wrong. I had no idea that she was going to leave me with an adult I didn't know, let alone make me face other children I'd never met. Living on a rural farm, we had no close neighbors, so my friends were my family, cows, pigs, and a few chickens. A room full of children was new territory and scared me to death.

I attended a rural school facility that was nationally recognized for its curricular and architectural stature, which only added to my fear. In the early twentieth century, our poor community was fortunate to have philanthropist William H. Miner as a resident. This man built a groundbreaking school system that was the pride of the country. The building was truly incredible, with twenty-foot ceilings, chandeliers, marble entrances, and a clock tower. Ironically, this historical school that caused me such fear would be the subject of a documentary I would produce and direct in 2002.

On that first day of kindergarten, Diane held my hand as we walked through the majestic school hallways. When my kindergarten teacher, Mrs. Miller, struggled to pry me away from my sister, I screamed and cried like never before. One thing was for sure, my earlier prediction that fear would revisit me had been more than accurate.

Mrs. Miller finally succeeded in dragging me into her room, but not for long. I wasn't there for more than ten minutes before the teacher turned her back and I ran out into the hallway, screaming for my sister. Discovering my exit and unaffected by my tears, Mrs. Miller hauled me back to class. My entrance into education was not going to be pretty. In that first year, I spent much of my time sitting behind Mrs. Miller's piano, her place for fearful children to take a time out.

I was not considered a good student. My mind was always elsewhere, and I was more interested in the proverbial "big picture" than math and science. In college, my psychology professor told me that when a student is being taught, the instructor's objective should be to convey the meaningfulness of the subject matter. If a student finds a subject interesting and meaningful, he will learn better.

Most of my elementary school teachers were unable to do this for me. In their notes, they referred to me as a "daydreamer." I could barely read by the middle of first grade, when I overheard a discussion about placing me in Special Education. Although I liked the idea of being "special," I was not happy about the potential classification. My classmates teased the kids in Special Education, and I didn't want to be the target of such attention. Sitting behind the piano was bad enough.

I was worried that Special Education was in my future, and I didn't know how to avoid a decision that adults would make for me. Around that time, Diane gave me a book about a pony having a difficult time. Perhaps I related to the pony, but for whatever reason, the pictures in this book grabbed my attention and I wanted to hear the story. I took the book home and one of my siblings helped me read it. The pony's story was very meaningful to me, and soon, I could read every word in that book.

It wasn't much, but I was proud of my achievement. During the next Show and Tell period, I read my book to the class. That night during dinner, our phone rang; my teacher called my mother to celebrate the seeming miracle that occurred that day. When my mom hung up the phone, she was dancing. She was so happy and proud of me, and I was, too! That phone call and my mom's reaction made me feel so good about myself that I worked hard to become a good reader. My motivation probably had more to do with a desire to earn more compliments than it did with the importance of knowing how to read. The self-esteem boost was amazing. Although I didn't know what the word *ego* meant, I clearly had one, and like most egos, mine had a good appetite for compliments.

Even after this first big success, I was still a "big picture" type of child, and although I had become a good reader, math, history, and science still did not hold much meaning for me. I was able to comprehend the content that meant something to me, but didn't put much effort into the rest. I went through my elementary years as a C student. I wish I could say that my junior high and high school years were different, but they weren't. To understand my struggles, all one has to do is add the onslaught of puberty to a daydreaming, big-picture type of child, and you're left with a formula for high-level confusion.

TWO

The Back Burner Fills Up

"I would rather have a mind opened by wonder than one closed by belief."

—GERRY SPENCE

My experiences thus far had begun to teach me how important it was to pay attention to my thoughts and feelings. I did not always have the answers to the questions I pondered, nor did I always understand the question, but I always tried to consider them deeply. I wanted to understand life, and I always felt a little safer if I could grasp a view or perspective that resonated with me. If it didn't, I wouldn't be convinced about the message it held.

A notable example occurred one day in Catechism class. The priest was teaching the concept of original sin, and explained how we were all implicated in that sin. I remember thinking that not only was this deal unjust, but also was an insane premise. I felt that I couldn't have possibly wronged a God I didn't know. Moreover, I was expected to atone for this sin and behave a certain way if I wanted to return to Heaven. It seemed like spiritual salvation was going to be a lot of work and I wasn't sure I would be successful, especially in light of my academic history. The priest's teachings made no sense. The lesson did not resonate with me.

Contrary to my Catechism experience, I later heard that sin was simply an error to be corrected, rather than something to be punished. That message resonated with me. No one had to preach it or convince me; it just felt true. Unfortunately, this revelation occurred much later in my life, so I spent my younger years grappling with the notion of original sin. I was just a twelve-year-old boy dealing with puberty on one hand and the prospect of Hell on the other. I entered high school with these two issues as my primary concerns, and both had equal ability to steal my peace of mind.

As puberty hit, I quickly became the tallest in my family. I was nearly six feet tall, skinny, awkward, and somewhat uncoordinated. I had never been interested in sports, and even though my athletic brothers and sisters included me in all their games, I always suspected that it was just to make the teams even in number. Nevertheless, my new height gave me an edge in some sports, particularly basketball. My sisters Judy and Linda taught me some strategies and techniques, and I soon became a fairly decent basketball player. I had not expected to experience success in this area, but at this fragile point in my growth, I was happy to have something that could reinforce my self-esteem.

As the years went by, I became emotionally and sexually moved in ways that I did not understand or anticipate. My male friends garnered most of my attention, but I wasn't too concerned because I had been taught that boys eventually grew up to like girls. When I was thirteen, my brother showed me some pornographic pictures of girls he had stolen from our uncle's car. He asked me what I thought of them, and I replied honestly. I admitted that they were not interesting or arousing to me. Surprisingly, my usually angry brother recognized my innocent sincerity and reassured me. He insisted that I was still too young and not to worry, that my attraction to girls would likely happen within the year. He succeeded in easing my worry as to why my male friends were more appealing than girls were. I had faith that my brother was probably right, so I kicked my fear down the hall and simply waited to wake up one morning with a completely different view on the matter. It must have been a long hallway, because by the time I was sixteen, my feelings had not changed. In fact, I became even *more* interested in boys and began to fear that my attraction to boys was never going to change.

Although my grades weren't strong, I wasn't stupid. I had learned enough in health class to be aware of homosexuality. In the 1970s, homosexuality was presented as a rare, psychological anomaly affecting only one percent of the world's population. Curing such an affliction is difficult, I was told. If health class wasn't enough to amplify my anxiety, my lessons in catechism classes made it clear that when a man lies with a man, it is an abomination. Everything I learned made me realize that I had some obstacles ahead of me. I didn't feel that I had done anything wrong or purposefully created the problem, but I knew I would have to face these issues nonetheless.

My current situation gave me a plethora of emotions to review. I felt fear, embarrassment, anger, disappointment, and frustration. I was afraid that my family would no longer love me and would be embarrassed that I could never live up to their expectations. Despite what some people told me, I didn't choose to have these feelings, and I was angry that God would make me this way. My life was going to be complicated.

It seemed tremendously unfair that I should fall into this shameful one percent, and I was disappointed and frustrated that there appeared to be no solution for me. If my leg became infected with a fatal case of gangrene, I could at least cut it off. There was no cutting off homosexuality. The only solution to this impossible situation was the closet, for it is indeed the place we put things we don't want others to see. I accepted this necessary but regrettable solution. I came to terms with my sexuality, and I thought that maybe if I could survive being gay, there could be nothing else in the world that would generate such fear and anger within me. Like so many other things, I was wrong about that speculation, too. There were still plenty of troubles and traumas in my future, and when they finally arrived, I began to realize that being gay didn't earn me a "Get Out of Jail Free" card. Suffering one day doesn't mean you won't also suffer the next.

Although staying the closet was essential to my survival, I still had the same hopes and desires as every other teenager, and I worried that most of them would never be fulfilled. I wasn't just concerned about finding sexual intimacy, but like any young person, I had dreams of falling in love. Much of my pain stemmed from the fear that finding love would be nearly impossible for me. Even if I were lucky enough to stumble across another "rare homosexual," what were the chances that we would be compatible? Even if we were, how could I share our union with society, let alone my family and friends? I began to understand why some people jump off bridges, but death scared me even more than being gay. Still, the fact that some people choose suicide instead of coping with judgment from others illustrates how fear can cause us to take truly irrational measures. Some may argue that hiding in the closet was just as irrational, but the world was very different back in 1972.

I ruled out the bridge as a coping method, and instead chose the closet as my first line of defense. My second line of defense was more proactive and involved one of my few academic skills: reading. I read and studied everything I could on the subject of homosexuality. I was relieved to read some progressive articles that argued we are born with our sexuality already determined, that the gay population was closer to ten percent, and that the word *perverted* did not accurately describe people like me.

This comforting new information was counterbalanced by the theological assertion that, at best, being homosexual was not a sin but "behaving" as a homosexual was, and that participating in a physical relationship with the same gender was a first-class ticket to Hell. My religious education told me that I could love someone of the same gender, but I could never touch him. That lesson was enough for me to discard what religion was teaching. I refused to believe that a loving God would put me in my situation and then condemn me for it. I refused to forfeit a happy, loving relationship. After all, I only wanted the same intimacy and love that we all crave. If Hell is the cost, I was prepared pay it.

Once I had made that decision, I put my worries about eternity on the back burner. The remainder of my high school years continued in the same way: I earned moderate grades, played some sports, and tried to come up with excuses as to why I was not dating. My fears of being outed permeated my everyday life, and I had to constantly ensure that my cloaking devices were activated. My peers used words like *faggot* and *queer* in jest and insult, and each word flung made me cringe. I discovered that in the locker room, heterosexual, high school boys have a tendency to jokingly ask other boys to "suck their dick."

As a gay teenager, I was filled with fear and excitement when other boys made sexual remarks to me. I was excited at the thought that maybe they were gay, too, but the thought that perhaps they saw through me and knew what I was terrified me. I never had the courage to act on their comments, but these locker room conversations only added to my feelings of confusion. All I could do was try to understand the world around me, and such understanding did not come fast or easy.

I couldn't comprehend how so much hypocrisy and judgment toward the gay community could exist in politics, religion, and society, and the latent homosexual comments my peers made did little to further my understanding of sexual expression. Even more, I wanted to know what love was all about. My mind and heart were burdened with heavy matters, and since it seemed that a deeper, comprehensive understanding was beyond my reach, I put them on the back burner. I figured that I just needed to survive high school and hoped that somehow my world would change once I was in the "real world." The rest of high school was a struggle, both academically and personally, but I continued to practice the art of pretending to be straight. In June of 1975, I received my high school diploma, and that fall, I enrolled in a local community college.

Perhaps it was a cosmic joke, but that same year, my family rediscovered Jesus Christ. I thought things couldn't get worse. Thanks to Jimmy and Tammy Faye Baker and their infamous television show, the *Praise The Lord Club*, my family joined the Evangelical movement.

I believe that in one way or another, everyone connects with their inner spirituality at some point in their lives, and I think it is a healthy thing to do. Many people use organized religion to reach spiritual enlightenment, but it might serve them better to look within. I have discovered that religions with specific doctrines have a tendency to view some people as separate or different, which makes it very difficult to be inclusive. If we are to be a part of a religious group, we should do so with our eyes open. When I see any religion that has a need for people to change in order to be loved and accepted it gives me serious reason to pause.

However, in 1976, I failed to consider any pause. Like my family, I joined the Evangelical movement. I had only recently resigned myself to the cost of Hell in order to be fully human, but I still had an underlying belief that Jesus's message had been misunderstood. If I could discover some biblical text, some wording that was contrary to what I had been taught, then maybe my future intimate relationships wouldn't come at such a high cost. My friends and family pressured me to join the evangelical church, and when coupled with my desire to gain a deeper understanding of scripture, I chose to step into that world.

In the years that I was involved with this charismatic religious movement, I felt like a zebra disguised as a lion. I walked amongst the pride, but I was constantly worried about being discovered and devoured. My participation lasted through college but as much as I tried, I never felt like I truly belonged. I couldn't bring myself to accept the preached belief of the rapture – the moment when all the saved souls ascend to Heaven to be with God. Many of the church's practices seemed more like voodoo to me, such as speaking in tongues or being "slain in the spirit," where members have hands laid on them and collapse to the floor.

I felt very disconnected, and the spiritual comfort I hoped to find never materialized. My family and friends still considered me a "reborn Christian" despite my misgivings, and I continued to try because I wanted to give religion every chance I could. With that goal in mind, after two years of community college, I decided to obtain my bachelor's degree in Physical Education from a Christian college. If a preacher couldn't comfort me or satisfy my intellectual curiosity about God, then maybe a professor of theology could.

Again, I was wrong.

Bible study, Christian doctrine, and other courses failed to answer many of my questions, especially regarding the origin of evil. Did God know ahead of time that Eve would pick the apple? How could a divine, perfect God create anything that *wasn't* inherently perfect? College also failed to provide me with any contrary information regarding the traditional views of homosexuality. I grew increasingly frustrated and resigned myself to the reality that I was bound for Hell.

Just as I was ready to give up, I learned a lesson that would be more painful and difficult than any of my courses: I fell in love. His name was Bill. He was my closest friend, but he was straight. First love is a confusing vortex that ensnares almost every young person and I was no different. In 1978, however, a young gay male falling in love with a young straight male, could be better described as a black hole.

I hadn't expected to fall in love with Bill; it just happened. When I realized that I had, it startled me and I remember thinking, "So this is what love is like." Bill did not know about my feelings, but I was sure he would notice, given the amount of time I made sure to spend with him. What he did notice, however, were my mood swings. When he finally asked me about them, I wasn't sure how to respond, so I suggested we go for a ride and talk.

As Bill drove my 1975 Chevrolet Malibu down New York's Taconic Parkway, I sat in the passenger seat, filled with fear. Finally, we found a space in a dimly lit parking lot and Bill turned off the car. After a few minutes of small talk, I summoned up every ounce of courage I could muster and told him the whole truth. I could see disbelief rush over his face, but his reaction was empathetic. He spoke about the pain I must have experienced as a child. He didn't know what to say or do, but that didn't matter to me. It just felt so good to have someone know the truth about me and not judge me for it.

When you grow up being told that you are perverted, queer, and going to Hell, it is difficult not to judge yourself, and equally difficult to believe that others won't judge you. On an unconscious level, I couldn't believe that Bill could accept me for who I truly was. Even though his kindness and caring seemed authentic, I didn't know how to trust it. My need for constant reassurance that he cared for me eventually sabotaged my friendship with him. He came to see that his involvement with me was hurting me more than helping me, so he stepped away. When he left, it felt like I had killed my savior. The pain and sense of loss over the end of my friendship with Bill showed me the true meaning of the word *anguish*. So, while home on Christmas break, I confided in Linda and told her the whole story.

I needed a lifeline so badly, but it wasn't easy. Coming out to her was one of the most difficult things I've ever done. I worried about causing her pain or heartache, but I no longer had any choice. I sat on the rocking chair in our living room, but wasn't sure Linda would be able to make me smile this time. I bit the bullet and told her the truth. It was like vomiting a bad meal: hard to do and messy, but when you're done, you feel better. When I finished my confession, I sat quietly and waited for her reaction. Like Bill, Linda did not blink or act surprised. I had been worried all my life about people knowing who I was, so it was astonishing that the first two people I told reacted as if I had only informed them that it was raining.

Like a well-trained pilot learning that an engine has gone out, Linda accepted the information and made appropriate adjustments to continue flying. I don't remember exactly what she said to me that night, but I know that I felt loved and accepted. I have never asked her what she was feeling or thinking as I talked, but she never showed her cards. It's not surprising that she is a very good poker player. Linda helped me through this difficult time and I wonder if she knew that she would have many more opportunities to comfort me in times of despair in the years to come.

It was finally clear that college would not reveal any hidden scriptures that would give me permission to be who I was. More importantly, those years gave me my first glimpse into how hard it can be to be honest with the people you love. My first brush with young love likely mirrored most, in that it didn't last. I had been needy, manipulative, controlling, jealous, and angry – everything that love isn't supposed to be. Why had I behaved that way? I was only twenty-one, but there were a lot of questions on my plate and no answers. Nonetheless, I still had dreams to fulfill and hormones to satisfy. Life was ahead for me, and it called to me more than my philosophical questions did. I'd have to learn to keep many issues on the back burner.

THREE

Small Lessons Can Teach Us Big Things

"Your pain is the breaking of the shell that encloses your understanding."

—KAHLIL GIBRAN

Simply put, pain comes to us when things don't go our way. The world is our shell and we work very hard to manage people and circumstances. When we fail, our shell fractures and we experience pain. This pain can be a useful tool, because the fracture makes us want to understand how pain can be better managed and how peace might be achieved.

Like everyone else, I've never liked emotional pain. I didn't know how to exist with it, and for much of my life, I'd done everything I could to avoid it. It never occurred to me that my pain could be telling me something, but it was. When I realized that I would always be gay or that I could not prevent my mother's death, I knew that I would have to find a way to live with these fears and cope with them. Approaching pain differently was a process because my inherent need to do things my way made it difficult for me to consider another. Pain is a great motivator, however, and over time, my shell began to show cracks.

In February of 1980, I got a job at the Winter Olympics in Lake Placid as a VIP chauffeur. I remember applying for the position, not fully understanding what VIP stood for. When I learned that it was an acronym for a *Very Important Person*, my first instinct was to wonder if I was less important than the people I'd be driving. I felt aggravated that some people believed themselves to be more important than others, and that I didn't seem to be one of the important ones. Medical personnel at an accident scene were "important," and in such an environment, those individuals would be needed and therefore more important than, say, a professional golfer at the same scene. But this was different. It was my sense that the people I drove had been identified as more "special" than I was. This bothered me deeply, and the knowledge that we are all destined for the same end did not make me feel any better.

Later that year, I got a job aboard a Russian cruise liner named for the famous Russian poet Alexander Pushkin. The ship docked in Montreal and sailed to various destinations along the St. Lawrence River and the North Atlantic. I was assistant to the Cruise Director, and part of my job was to greet passengers in the main salon once we embarked. I wore my most formal attire to meet the excited travelers who stood in line to shake my hand.

The shoe had been placed on the other foot – I felt so special and important. How ironic that only a few months earlier, in the cold Adirondacks, I felt like a servant for the important people. If I had viewed my situation in Lake Placid from a different perspective, I could have been proud that I was an employee of the 1980 Winter Olympics, but instead, I chose to feel sorry for myself. Four months later, aboard the ship, nothing fundamental had changed. I was still the same person, and only the situation was new.

It made little sense that the outside world should determine my self-worth or my state of being, but it did. Therefore, it seemed reasonable that I should hold the world responsible for my pain as well as my pleasure. I knew that this wasn't a healthy attitude, but I didn't have the tools necessary to adjust my mindset. I resigned myself to my lot in life. This self-reflection would be followed by a lifetime of exploring the world and my place in it, and would eventually result in a deeper understanding of what it really means to experience feelings.

When my job on the cruise ship ended at the end of the summer, I moved to New York City. In the days before the Internet, many young, gay men moved to urban centers to improve their chances of meeting someone like themselves. Interested to see what the world had in store for me, I joined the herd.

With my degree in hand, I got a job at a weight training facility near the United Nations. This gym served mostly men, and more than half of them were gay. I was so naïve that it took me at least six months to realize how many of our clients were like me. I liked exercising, but I thought I was the exception within the gay community. I mistakenly believed that most gay men did not go to the gym.

Perhaps my stereotypes were developed from watching early Hollywood films, which portrayed homosexuals as sissies with feminine traits, lacking in courage, and possessing little to no athletic ability. I took these portrayals as factual and assumed that the average gay man did not play sports or have any interest in working out at a gym.

Looking back, I'm amazed that I didn't see the signs. Barbara Streisand and Donna Summer blared loudly over the sound of clacking barbells, and there were rarely any women around. Like so many other moments in my life, it took me time to notice what was right in front of me.

As I settled into life in New York, I felt increasingly comfortable as a member of the gay community. I frequented gay nightclubs and felt at home at my gym and on the streets. Slowly, I realized that the conservative or religious articles I'd read that claimed homosexuals only represented one percent of the population had been terribly wrong. The stereotype that gay men are puny, feminine, and weak was misleading. I felt badly that I had bought the lie without question. Putting my guilt aside, it was comforting to realize that there was a sizeable population that endured the same challenges I faced and had survived.

I enjoyed working at the gym and found it interesting that the owner was straight, as was the manager. I'm sure they knew that most of their members were gay, but they either tolerated it for financial reasons or it simply didn't matter to them. Whatever the reason, it was reassuring to see that not every heterosexual man felt threatened by a homosexual one. The owner, Tim, was a very fit, fifty-year-old man who commuted into the city from Westchester. Tony, his manager, was the quintessential Italian from Brooklyn. Both men were married. Their behavior introduced me to aspects of sex and love that I hadn't previously considered.

Raised with traditional values, I had a limited understanding of modern intimate relationships. Intellectually, I understood that a person could have sex without being in love, but I assumed that such relationships were rare. My Catholic and Evangelical upbringing taught me that sex and love were always correlated, and I believed what I'd been told. Though I knew I probably would never be married, I assumed that I would meet someone one day, date, and live my life with him, *monogamously* and happily ever after. It is amazing how often I can be wrong.

Tony was the first to make me examine the difference between sex and love. One night, as the gym was closing and I was about to head home, Tony instructed me to leave the door unlocked. Before I could ask why, he excitedly told me that one of the girls who worked out at the gym was coming back and he was going to "screw her" over the roman bench.

Unable to contain my shock, I reminded Tony that he was married, as if he had forgotten. He seemed confused by my innocence and responded in a way only a gold-chain-wearing, muscle-bound, Italian Brooklynite could. He said, "Rick, ya dick don't fall off when you get married, ya know!"

I had to step back and digest this simple truth. Before I could gather my thoughts or a response, Tony claimed that he loved his wife, that he would never want to lose her, and that if I should tell her of his indiscretion, he would certainly kill me. I had no doubt that his threat was genuine, so I reassured him that his wife would hear nothing from me. On the way home, I thought about nothing but Tony and his roman bench girl. It was incredible to me that Tony was able to separate sex and love in such a distinct way. Millions of questions raced through my mind, including the age-old belief that one person should be everything for you and how unfair this was to Tony's wife. This was tricky territory. Tony spoke of his wife all the time, and I really believed that he loved her completely. I was dumbfounded by the possibility that one could have sex with someone they did not love, especially while being in love with another.

I was twenty-one years old, and my sex drive was a moving force kept in check only by the values I had been taught. The episode with Tony caused me to reconsider *everything* I believed regarding sex, love, and relationships. It was simply too much for me to process. I wasn't sure if Tony was the norm or the anomaly, but I had a difficult time understanding the concept of sex without love, so I tried to put it out of my mind.

I couldn't ignore the matter for long. When I was hired, I noticed that the owner continuously ran a posting for a secretary in the Village Voice. On a weekly basis, girls came in to interview in response to the ad. Fifteen minutes after their arrival, Tim left his office, picked up a towel from the locker room, returned to his office, and locked the door. When his office door opened again, the young woman would exit, looking disheveled. I foolishly believed that her tousled appearance meant that she didn't get the job and was upset.

I finally asked Tony why Tim never hired anyone, and he said, "What? You stupid? Tim pays those girls and screws them in his office. The classified ad is just a front!" I was shocked and it occurred to me that perhaps my C-average in school was deserved. Again, I had found myself facing something as big as an elephant but had failed to see it. What else had I missed?

Despite my embarrassment and confusion, I stayed on with the gym for about a year and ultimately recovered from the idea of Tony on the roman bench and Tim conducting interviews. I learned a few things about weight training, but the lesson that stuck with me most was that sex and love were two different things and their relationship may not have been what I believed.

The gym closed in 1982 and I landed a position providing physical recreation at a small school for special needs children in Brooklyn. I was offered the job thanks in part to the recommendation of a very good friend named Ted, a former client of the gym. He was a short, overweight, hairy, secular Jew with a very high voice. His appearance and personal style were so unique that I was surprised he wasn't a character actor in Hollywood. His sense of humor, street smarts, and insights made me laugh and feel safe, so I found it easy to be friends with him.

Ted was a psychologist at a Brooklyn hospital, but at night, he managed several strip clubs owned by a man named Jack. Jack owned strip clubs in midtown Manhattan, Washington D.C., and Pittsburgh. Because of Ted's involvement with these clubs, I learned a lot about a business that I never would have experienced otherwise. My peek into this world furthered my understanding of what a breaking shell can reveal.

One weekend, Jack flew Ted and me to Pittsburgh for the Mardi Gras celebration at his club. His establishment was located in a huge building in a remote and depressing part of Pittsburgh. The upper level catered to the gay community and featured male dancers, while the lower level was a traditional strip club with female dancers for heterosexual men. The lower level was larger and included a stage with a runway down the center of the room, as if the dancers planned to put on a fashion show.

That weekend, I spent my time upstairs, helping Ted with decorations and watching men my age dance naked on a small stage as entertainment for the visitors. Sometimes after the performance, a stripper would lead a paying and eager customer into a curtained booth for a "private dance." Contrary to my usual naiveté, I knew exactly what was going on and found myself feeling very judgmental of these gay men.

That Saturday night, Ted and I went downstairs to watch the girls dance. Approximately three hundred men howled and cheered as thirty girls put on a special show for the special weekend. The men were shouting louder than at a football game as barely dressed erotic dancers pranced around. I was not surprised at their enthusiasm, but what did shock me was that as each dancer approached the end of the stage, she removed what clothing was left and allowed man after man to perform oral sex on her. Stunned at such a public sexual display, I began to think that perhaps my judgment of the gay men upstairs had been too harsh.

With such images burned into my brain forever, the issues of sex and love reemerged in my mind. I knew that my emotional reactions stemmed from my conservative upbringing, but even with that realization, it was still difficult for me to avoid thoughts of sin when sex was had in a way that didn't conform to religious doctrine. It may sound strange for a gay man to speak of religious sexual morality, especially when any sexual act I would perform would be against most religious teaching, but when one is raised and taught a certain way, it is very difficult to reverse embedded lessons and expectations.

My previous experiences with Tony and Tim coupled with my weekend at this Sodom and Gomorrah of a strip club compelled me to reevaluate my positions on sex, love, and sin and how they intertwined. I did believe that Tony and Tim loved their wives, and as I watched the men cheer for the girls on stage, they didn't seem to be sinful but were simply having fun. Everyone visiting Jack's club was an adult, engaging in harmless and consensual sexual experiences. I began to wonder what the harm was, and wondered if going to a baseball game was any different from going to a strip club.

I gradually began to understand that sex was something physical, like breathing, eating, or sleeping. These actions are not *love* any more than they are *sin* – they are simply things we do. It occurred to me that a man having intercourse with his wife could be loving, yet a man forcing the same act on a woman would not be. I began to realize that *why* we do something is perhaps more important than *what* we do.

This new perspective helped me feel better about myself because it led me to consider that if sex wasn't a sin, neither was I. My shell fractured a little bit that weekend and a new understanding spilled through: everything I had ever been taught about love and sin could be wrong. It was just a hairline fracture and the understanding that emerged was minimal. Deep within, I still wanted to understand the real purpose of our lives, but I wasn't sure that I ever would.

Through my experiences as a chauffeur, my job on the cruise ship, Tony and Tim at the gym, and now Pittsburgh, it seemed that I was chipping away at the marble. Very slowly, I began to appreciate that the way I choose to view my world will have a direct effect on how I feel about it. This insight was underscored not long after I returned to New York. Walking with Ted down 44th Street, I complained about how I needed to get a birthday card for a friend. I whined for three blocks about how I hadn't found one that I liked, that they seemed expensive, and that going to the post office to get a stamp would be a headache. By the fifth block, Ted responded in only the way Ted could. He pointed his chubby finger at me and with his high, squeaky voice, he said, "Rick, when it is my birthday, if getting me a card is this much work, don't get me one!" I was completely embarrassed. I tried to backpedal, but it was too late. Ted had made his point. There really was no love involved in getting a birthday card for my friend. I was motivated by pure guilt.

When you love someone and you do something for him or her, no matter how difficult it might be, there is no sense of effort involved. You help because you *want* to, not because you *have* to. I was buying a card for someone because I was worried about how it would look if I didn't get the card. I wanted to appear kind and thoughtful, but my actions had nothing to do with the person celebrating a birthday. I wasn't being loving, I was being selfish, and so finding a birthday card became a chore.

That single remark from Ted made me reexamine my motivations and drove home the point that our motives can be more important than our actions. Indeed, it is not the gift, but the giving that matters. I began to inspect my behavior and realized that nearly everything I did was selfishly driven. Ordinarily, I like revelations, but this one hit a little too close to home. It was hard for me to accept that I was such a selfish person, but at least I could stop fooling myself into thinking I was Mother Teresa.

I wish I could say that Ted's remark propelled me into total spiritual understanding, but it didn't work that way. There is often resistance to accepting the truth that comes when our shell fractures, because such moments can turn our lives upside down. It took me another thirty years of pain and egotism to accept the fact that I'm afraid of understanding the world and myself. I'm still afraid.

I once read that Idries Shah said enlightenment must come little by little otherwise it would overwhelm us. Enlightenment has come slowly for me, and any enlightenment I have obtained has been achieved through looking, questioning, and a considerable amount of pain. If we weren't so afraid of the truth, becoming aware would be quicker and much less painful, but our fear holds us back. Coming to accept that our identity or self-worth has nothing to do with gender, age, money, intelligence, or sexuality is no small feat because we have forgotten our true nature and are convinced that we are bodies in a world of time. Our self-identity is misplaced and rooted in our ego consciousness, and not in our spiritual awareness so it seems natural for us to think that the world will provide the love and peace we seek, when in truth the world can never do this.

The world may provide a carrot now and then in the form of a new car, money, or a lover, but these things never truly last. Our lives are not a dream, but a nightmare from which we must gently awaken by examining our thoughts and looking at our fears. We can't concern ourselves with complete understanding, for it will come in time.

Just as Dorothy found her way along the yellow brick road, so shall we. Like Dorothy, we will awaken to a home we never truly left, but until we do, the Wicked Witch of the West will appear in the form of difficult relationships, illness, or sorrow. If Dorothy had truly understood that these things could not harm her, the yellow brick road would have been a more peaceful journey for her.

I have met more than one witch and even a few warlocks. They came to me disguised as difficult relationships, financial troubles, illness, and death. They made my life more challenging, but I learned from them. Each one fractured my shell a little more, and now I'm less afraid of hearing it crack.

FOUR

The Gay Nightclub

"The readiness to initiate the journey cannot be forced nor can people be faulted if it has not occurred in them as yet. The level of consciousness has to have advanced to the stage where such an intention would be meaningful and attractive."

—David R. Hawkins

On one level or another, everyone recognizes that life is a journey. It is the proverbial journey into the remembrance of our true nature, and it bears repeating that our true nature really does frighten us. Being human is attractive to us. We like the world we live in. We think the world will give us what we need to be happy, and we believe that the world has made us. We are completely unaware that it is *we* who made the world. We have it backwards. We are the authors of the dream, and in time, it will serve us to stop identifying with the character we have made on this stage.

We must come to a place where we recognize that the world is a dead end, and until we do, we won't take the first step on the journey that David Hawkins refers to in the above quote. Until that shift in our perception occurs, our lives will serve as a distraction from our true purpose. Distraction is not necessarily a bad thing, but it does indicate that we are not ready to begin our journey. Our fear merely delays us in time, nothing more.

When a young child stands at the edge of a pool, fearful of the unknown water, he should not be faulted for being afraid, nor should he be pushed. Pushing him before he's ready will incite panic and even more fear. It is better and kinder to let him get his feet wet. We are all like children, and our pool of water is awareness of our perfect oneness. To get our feet wet, we must advance our consciousness. It is important to not underestimate how rooted we have become in the notion that our bodies determine our identities. Suddenly reversing this mindset would be no different from being pushed into the deep end of the pool. If we let ourselves go slowly, the water will become familiar, our consciousness will rise, and we will be ready to hear the truth about ourselves. This process takes time. When I was a younger man in my early twenties, my consciousness was low and I often foolishly jumped in the deep end without knowing how to swim.

In the summer of 1982, I began a relationship with a man named Gary, though I knew from the beginning that I wasn't in love with him. When I met him, I believe that he was on a spiritual detour and was not ready to look within to seek spirituality. I met Gary at a bar in Greenwich Village, where we chatted about mundane things. When it was time for me to go home, he offered to give me a ride. I explained that I lived just a few blocks away, but he insisted. We walked to his car, a new BMW, and I commented on what a beauty it was. He defensively replied that I should not like him just because of his car. I expected him to just say "thank you" to my compliment, so I was taken aback by his defensive comeback. His response raised a red flag about his personality, but I didn't pay much attention. When he called me the next day, I agreed to meet him for dinner, and within three weeks, we were a couple. I remember wondering how a relationship could begin so quickly and how I became involved with someone so fundamentally different from me in the first place.

In hindsight, I can see that Gary pursued me with the cunning of a fox and the hunger of a grizzly. Even though I was somewhat aware of his tactics and manipulation, I overlooked them because it felt good to have someone want me so badly. It is difficult to admit the kind of excuses I made in order to maintain what I intellectually knew was a bad relationship. Yet, to have somebody pursue me was such a powerful high for my ego that all sensible decision-making abilities flew out the window.

To make our relationship work, Gary used his best tools: manipulation and control. From the start, I could see that he was a skilled manipulator and I knew that this couldn't possibly be the way to build a healthy relationship. Even so, I chose to stay involved with him. I can't blame Gary for our four years of hell because if our relationship was a crime, I was clearly an accomplice.

Gary loved to wield his power in the relationship, and added a splash of arrogance for good measure. Everyone around me saw it, and few had patience for him. Gary frequently made remarks that clearly showed his bigotry towards African Americans, and it astonished me that a gay man who knew what it felt like to be judged could so easily discriminate against others. I made efforts to show him the inconsistency and hypocrisy of his views, but he refused to listen. As the old expression goes,

"There are none so blind as those who will not see."

Eventually, Gary became a mission for me. I had the grandiose yet mistaken belief that I could change him, and if I were successful, I would not only improve our relationship but also honor how powerful I was. I failed on both counts. I now understand that it is not my duty to change anybody; true change can only come from within. I needed to work on myself, but instead, I forged ahead with our dysfunctional relationship. If we were playing a soccer game, I was losing the match at halftime. I still had a chance to win, which meant changing Gary.

As the second half of our game played out, Gary scored first by persuading me to quit teaching and go into business with him. I wasn't sure if it was the right thing to do, but he convinced me that I would never make much money from teaching, and in order to get what I wanted in life, I needed wealth. I accepted his proposition, but not because I believed that money was the path to happiness. Rather, it was the intangible things that money could buy that attracted me. From a young age, my poor academic history and my sexual orientation permeated my sense of self. I felt inadequate, not good enough, and judged. Wealth symbolized success, and perhaps success would mean that maybe I really am good enough. If Gary was right and we were able to obtain financial success, it might help make a dent in my low self-esteem. I had so little self-worth that I wrongfully assumed that everyone thought the worst of me for any number of reasons – my weak academic record, my lack of material wealth, my sexuality – everything I was ashamed of about myself. So, when Gary found an established gay nightclub for sale in Connecticut, I agreed to be his business partner.

Desperate to improve other's perceptions of me, I glossed over the fact that we purchased a *gay* nightclub. I assumed that

I could somehow avoid mentioning that part to people. When my parents (the people whose opinion mattered most) decided to drive all the way from upstate New York to see my new business, I had a dilemma to face. Although the rumor within my family was that I was gay, I was also quite certain that my mom and dad had not heard the whispers. In fact, my parents had a difficult time even saying the word *homosexual*.

When I was young and the subject of homosexuality came up on the nightly news, their uneasiness with the topic was obvious. It was beyond their scope of comprehension, and my siblings and I understood this. To shield them from undue discomfort, I suspect that my brothers and sisters had chosen to avoid the topic of my sexuality with my parents. This perceived judgment made their planned visit to my newly purchased nightclub a nerve-racking occasion. My sense of pride quickly evaporated. I didn't know how I was going deal with this impending disaster of my parents' visit. Once they saw my nightclub, I knew that I'd have to tell them the truth about my sexuality. Like any good ostrich, I put my head in the sand.

Luckily, my brother in law recognized that I was in complete denial about the looming visit. Instead of allowing my parents to be shocked into oblivion upon their arrival in Connecticut, he told them that at my club, the "men dance with the men, and the women dance with the women." Apparently, my parents were not the only ones who could not say the word *homosexual*. Nevertheless, even after they learned that their son most likely danced with men and not women, my parents chose to make the trip to Connecticut anyway.

When they arrived at my home, we exchanged hugs and pleasantries. The elephant in the room made me completely uncomfortable, but I clung desperately to my denial. But even denial has its limits, and before long, my mother broke the silence.

As expected, she never used the words *homosexual* or *gay*, but simply said that she had "heard" about everything, and that she and my dad loved me anyway. She continued to speak, but her words were like voices playing on a TV in the distance: I could hear the sound, but couldn't focus on the words. I was feeling exposed and shameful and I just wanted the conversation to end. Her assertion that she and my dad loved me "anyway" was comforting, but her words still gave me the feeling that I had committed a crime, that I was somehow guilty of something. I don't mean to diminish their support for me as their gay son, but their decision to continue to love me was the most they could give. Helping me deal with the shame and guilt of being gay was beyond their capability.

They were both born into Catholic families on rural farms near the turn of the century. When they were young, subjects such as divorce were taboo and only whispered about. I presume that conversations about homosexuality were nonexistent, so they never fully understood it. In fact, they told me so. Their supportive words that day were helpful, but I knew it would take something more than them telling me they "loved me anyway" to ease my guilt and shame. In any case, as coming out experiences go, I can't say that mine was a bad one. To this day, some parents disown their children when they come out. It was 1983 and my parents hadn't turned their backs on me; it could have been a much more painful experience, but it wasn't. For that, I am so thankful.

When Gary began the discussion about purchasing the nightclub, I should have seen the signs of disaster coming, but foresight has never been my strength. I should have predicted that Gary's tendency to control and manipulate would carry over into his business methodology. As we put together a financial portfolio to obtain bank loans, he was completely comfortable exaggerating our personal financial documents in ways that would have made any accountant cringe. His personality, a misleading portfolio, and other dirty tricks ultimately resulted in our successful acquisition of the nightclub. Within three months, our cash flow had more than quadrupled.

I saw little of the cash. The nightclub was a gold mine, but Gary took control of the entire business, including all the money. Essentially, my only role was to act as a sort of First Lady, but as good as I was at it, it wasn't enough to help the business continue in its historic success. Unfortunately, Gary couldn't help but be himself. His judgment of the patrons was obvious, and his need to eradicate every suspected drug dealer resulted in an empty dance floor and a ninety percent drop in cash flow.

Gary's solution to the downfall of our business was to run away from the lease, move to a different state using money he had hidden, and start over. My solution was to find my voice. Summoning courage I didn't know I had, I contacted an attorney, changed the locks on the club, and got my own apartment. To say Gary was furious would be an understatement; to say I was terrified would be a bigger one. The level of stress, disappointment, and fear I felt were extreme and I wasn't giving any thought to my spiritual journey. In fact, I wasn't even sure that I was on a journey.

The kindness, support, and lack of judgment from family and friends got me through this horrible time. I reminded myself that there are more serious things to endure than losing a business or the end of a dysfunctional relationship. There was surely the parent of a terminally ill child who would have traded places with me in a heartbeat.

Nonetheless, my pain and fear were *mine*, and I have come to appreciate that no one's hardship should be diminished or taken lightly. Linda once told me that when a child drops his treasured ice cream cone on the floor and cries, a loving parent reassures the child that everything will be okay and does not dismiss his tears. My loving friends and family did not dismiss mine. When it was all said and done, Gary followed through on his planned solution and I filed for bankruptcy reorganization. The club rebounded within a year and I had been handed a new ice cream cone. By 1985, life seemed good again. Regrettably, there is no forecast for life. There would undoubtedly be rain showers and bigger storms ahead for me, but at least for a while, the clouds had parted.

My sunny weather lasted for about a year and followed me as I led the single life, made money, and spent time with friends. I enjoyed a reprieve from personal drama and was easily able to observe the lives of those around me. A tremendously diverse group of people visited my nightclub, which made for fascinating people watching. My clientele ranged from rich to poor, famous to unknown, priests, doctors, sophisticated and polite, drunk and foolish, young, old, male, female and every race possible. By listening to their conversations and watching the behavior of such a diverse group, I learned that although we have our differences, we are the same in one particular way: we all seek love.

Many of my customers claimed that they only stopped in for a beer, but I saw through their charade. It is much cheaper to buy beer at the supermarket and take it home. People visited my club to socialize and meet new people. Many single people go out to meet others at nightclubs, ballgames, or operas, hoping to find another to satisfy their emotional needs. Yes, it is nice to have a drink out with friends or watch a homerun on a sunny afternoon, but we often go out to watch for that certain someone who will meet a need within us that we have been unable to fulfill ourselves. I am no different from anyone else in this respect, and the observations I've made about others could just as easily be made about me. When I was young, I was never able to figure out the root cause of my emotional needs, so instead, I focused simply on satisfying them. In the process, I met Ron.

Over the next thirteen years, Ron would serve as one of my biggest teachers, not necessarily due to his wise, amazing insights, but because he pushed my buttons like no one else could. When I met him, he was eighteen and I was twenty-seven; this alone should have given me pause and caused me to move slowly, but it didn't. I was immersed in my ego and he was cute, and that's often all it takes for two people to get involved at lightning speed.

Like any relationship, Ron and I had our ups and downs, and I have no desire to paint him as the bad guy. We all need a dance partner to play out our ego's tango, and with Ron, I was a willing participant and can place no blame. I prefer to compare our relationship to the 1956 cruise liner accident between the *Stockholm* and the *Andrea Doria* in New York Harbor. In the dense fog of ego and fear, we each blew our horns of caution at the same time, never hearing the other's call. Like those two fateful ships, we collided. Fortunately, neither of us sank.

Our first few years together were actually pretty good, but then again, they are for most relationships. People tend to hide their character flaws in the early stages of a relationship, and only when they believe they are fully committed do they feel safe enough to show their true selves. The expression, "You're not the person I married" is certainly true because we too often change from our dating self into our true self when we become comfortable or complacent in our relationships. Insecure people often worry that if they show exactly who they are, their partner would run away screaming. So, to get the relationship off the ground and to get the love we seek, we go to the gym a bit more, wear a little more makeup, and hide our flaws so that our partner won't leave or judge us…*at least* until we have them captured.

Ron had captured me after a year's time by being especially polite, quitting college, moving in with me, and working in my nightclub. Once we felt settled, he began to show parts of his personality that I'd never seen. Before I knew it, the polite, kind, non-judgmental person I was dating became an angry, controlling man who manipulated by provoking fear. Everyone battles feelings of guilt and fear, and these unconscious feelings are repressed and then projected on to others because we can't bear to face them within ourselves. Ron could project his fear better than Yankee pitcher Mariano Rivera could throw a cutter.

One Christmas season, I went with Ron, Linda, and a few of my friends to the mall for a little holiday shopping. We each went our separate ways and made plans to meet at the food court for lunch. Ron was a few minutes late, but the rest of us met as scheduled and talked excitedly about our enjoyable shopping experiences and the gifts we had purchased. When Ron arrived, he complained loudly about the myriad of idiots he had encountered. I quietly remarked to Linda how interesting it was that Ron was able to locate all the difficult shoppers. My observation startled me a little because it was one of the first times I recognized that we really do create the world around us. Our eyes can see impatient, hurried shoppers, or people excited about the holidays. We get to choose.

Ron's projection of fear of course included yours truly, and he always seemed overly comfortable yelling at me, embarrassing me, insulting me, or disagreeing with me on almost every front. I rarely felt comfortable discussing politics with him because he took any dissent as a threat to our relationship. So I held back. I avoided deep conversations with him; I made the excuse that it wasn't important, when really, I hoped to prevent an argument. In retrospect, I can't blame Ron for this. My own need to avoid conflict kept me quiet.

Our relationship continued onward, but I couldn't be honest with him and our communication suffered. Objectively, I knew this was a terrible formula for a relationship, but this dynamic was all too familiar. My relationship with Gary followed a similar path, and I had seen this dynamic in so many other relationships, both straight and gay. I began to wonder if all couples worked this way. I considered ending things, but I knew that would be the mother of all conflicts, so I chose to stay and deal with the smaller brush fires that Ron lit. My friends and family could see the flaws in our relationship and I was ashamed that I didn't have the courage to step away from someone who was in such a different emotional place than I was. To be fair, I must also say that I saw in Ron something that others didn't see. Even as Ron shot arrows at me, I sensed that he wasn't truly upset with me. I felt the pain of his anger, but I knew I wasn't the real target. This small insight helped me to not take his anger personally or view him as the bad guy. When I could, I made a conscious decision not to play into his drama, and I think that made Ron feel safe. It was difficult not to get caught up in the ego's dance, but whenever I succeeded, it was worth the effort.

Relating to another person is an art form, and it begins by realizing that as bad, fearful, or dysfunctional as they may seem, our response to their behavior is *our* responsibility. We cannot control how they act, but we can choose how we respond. I have said that Ron was on his spiritual detour, but so was I. My only real responsibility was and will always be to recognize that I'm accountable for how I view and understand the world and the people in it. All my relationships until that point, including Ron, had been challenging. Only when I was able to shift my thinking about how I was supposed to *be* in relation to my partner did they become less daunting.

It isn't easy to change our perspective because it feels so natural to see the world in black and white: good or bad, happy or miserable, them or us. An examination of mankind's history shows this to be true. My emotional neediness and perception of the world was the same as it was for men throughout history. Only the date has changed. The human climate of seeing differences in others, judging them, and holding others accountable for our feelings remains unchanged, and often, this perception and judgment of others is hypocritical.

For example, early Christians were viewed as different and were persecuted for their beliefs. How ironic, then, that in the 1980s, under the direction of the Catholic Church's Cardinal O'Connor, the rabbit chased the fox. Many Christians felt righteous in attacking and judging the gay community for their lifestyles and beliefs. In place of a wooden cross for crucifixion, the Catholic Church gave a nod to the likes of Senator Jesse Helms to obstruct any legislation that would grant equal rights to the gay community.

I watched this unfold at the national level, and even though I was making progress on how I reacted to Ron, it was hard for me not to feel persecuted and hated by the Church and legislators. Yet, to despise them would mean I was no different. I knew I had to reverse my thinking with Cardinal O'Connor and Senator

Helms just as I had done with Ron. If I had the ability to see through Ron's fear, then I could translate that ability to unmask everyone's fear. Still, talking the talk was easier than walking the walk, and even now, it can be difficult for me not to hold another person or the world accountable for my feelings. This was especially difficult as a young man, when I knew that Cardinal O'Connor's words and Senator Helms's actions motivated narrow-minded people to drive by my nightclub and shout *faggot* or throw beer bottles at me. Nonetheless, I did my best to remain calm. Even if the church and the government seemed to hate me, at least I knew that my mom and dad still loved me.

The 1970s and 1980s were a turbulent time for the gay community. We fought for equality while people like Jesse Helms, Anita Bryant, and Cardinal O'Connor fanned the flames of hatred. When the AIDS epidemic exploded, it seemed as if the proverbial final nail in the coffin had been hammered in. Surprisingly, such challenges united our community and brought us even closer together. I wanted do my part, and somehow, breaking up with Ron seemed like the wrong thing to do. I believed that staying with him would send the message that gay and lesbian people could succeed at having healthy, loving relationships, too.

My relationship with Ron was far from loving or healthy, but we weren't so different from the relationships around us, both gay and straight. So many people I knew fought the same battles we did. From where I was sitting, relationships were the same across the board, and no one group had a monopoly on the prescription for a loving relationship. In a strange way, my dysfunctional relationship with Ron made me part of the norm for change, and the irony of that didn't escape me.

FIVE

Do We Really Die?

"Death is one of two things. Either it is annihilation, and the dead have no consciousness of anything, or, as we are told, it is really a change – a migration of the soul from this place to another."

—SOCRATES

Many religions have been organized in the quest for a better understanding of what it means to live and die, and I believe that many of them have come to the wrong conclusions. Socrates speculated that death is a migration of the soul from one place to another, and I find that notion appealing, though I would word it differently. To me, death is simply another experience that can help to initiate the *remembering* of our soul, not the migration of it.

The psychological, spiritual text *A Course in Miracles* has had a significant influence on my life. It says that bodies do not die because they do not live. As much as we identify ourselves as bodily humans, the essence of our true nature is abstract and one with God. Nonetheless, death feels real to us, and knowing that death will approach us all with certain steps is a frightening prospect. It is little wonder why some refuse to consider their future bodily death and are only willing to address it when it knocks at their door.

Death's certain steps were heard on my sidewalk in 1987. It didn't knock on my door, but on Ron's. Ron's impending death was unexpected and distressing, but I've learned that *every* event we face can teach us something, and we can choose to respond in one of two ways: we can act like an ostrich and live in denial, or we can look deeper and discover our soul. If we choose to look deeper we will begin to realize that life's purpose is not to solve the world's problems but rather to use the worlds challenges as tools to help us awaken to our higher conscious. This is not to say that we shouldn't develop careers or build relationships, but these lower worldly purposes should be understood as mere mechanisms that allow us to choose the higher purpose of awakening to the remembrance of our true self. Worldly goals and ambitions are not the destination, but are vehicles that help us migrate to our soul, which *is* our ultimate destination.

It is undeniable that some life mechanisms are more difficult or longer-lasting than others. For a child, the mechanism is dropping their ice cream cone, and for an adult, it is the loss of a loved one. These experiences are quite different, but from a spiritual perspective, they both provide an opportunity to choose our response, and therefore, choose the path back to our soul. Therefore, we can find comfort in the knowledge that no matter how our lives unfold, how messy they become, we have within us the ability to make the right choice and spiritually grow.

When the AIDS epidemic emerged in the early eighties, much of the aforementioned philosophy could be found woven through the gay community's response to this crisis. When the epidemic took root, I feared that it would push the gay community back into the closet, but in fact, the opposite happened: it brought us closer together. It is difficult for me to describe how the gay community perceived the AIDS crisis with respect to *mindful purpose*, but as a group, they refused to put their heads in the sand. I witnessed an abundance of kindness and a unity of spirit that I will never forget.

Since I owned a gay nightclub in the pre-Internet days, my establishment quickly became a meeting point for those wishing to discuss this unknown, terrifying illness. Very little was known about this disease, and since ignorance quickly breeds panic and fear, those early years were frightening. AIDS was like Russian roulette, and no one knew who was up next.

In the next four years, I watched many patrons and friends lose weight and die. So many beautiful, talented, loving people passed away, and it broke my heart to hear some members of the religious community declare that this was God's scourge on the gay community. I found these assertions cruel and insane, and I imagined the additional pain that their heartless rhetoric brought to those grieving loved ones.

Nobody wanted to face the reality of the virus, but some things in life just can't be avoided. Ron and I decided to face the music and get tested for HIV. Time stood still when the doctor informed us that Ron was HIV-positive. The word *terror* doesn't begin to describe how afraid I was. As the doctor described Ron's options, the room spun and his voice became surreal. I vaguely heard him mention a drug called AZT, and he said that if Ron were able to tolerate it, he had a chance to survive for ten more years. Ron had been given a death sentence.

Even in my dreamlike state, I knew that Ron didn't have the skills to cope with the information we'd been given, so I made the conscious decision to put my feelings of dread on hold so I could help him deal with this. We had a lot to digest after we left the doctor's office that day, and we quickly made some decisions about how to respond to the news. First, we agreed that Ron would not take any medication. He was asymptomatic, and since the level of HIV in his body had not yet compromised his immune system, immediate medical action was not warranted. In those early days, few people were eager to take the AZT, which was controversial and notorious for its debilitating side effects. After weighing our options, Ron and I decided to take the "watch and see" approach to his medical treatment. Secondly, we both agreed to delay telling Ron's family about his diagnosis. I loved his family as much as he did, and we knew that neither of us could handle the added stress of witnessing their pain and tears. In fact, I insisted that we keep the news from everyone we knew until we could wrap our minds around it.

I kept a close eye on Ron to gauge how he was coping with his life-changing news. I had become very familiar with his tendency to internalize difficult situations he couldn't face and then project his fear and anger onto me. In this case, I didn't have to wait long before he unleashed his wrath.

The night we received the test results, we had a commitment in New York City that we couldn't avoid. That evening, we got into a fight on the streets of Manhattan, and when the fight turned physical, an off-duty police officer had to break it up. The ferocity of our brawl and Ron's anger made it clear that the catalyst was his diagnosis and not our petty argument. Nonetheless, the fight bothered me deeply, and I began to wonder if I had the strength and skills to help Ron through the battle he faced. Our relationship was strained enough without adding HIV to our list of challenges. After witnessing his burning anger and fear, our relationship shifted and we couldn't connect as we once did.

I found it difficult to be intimate with Ron, not because of the risk of HIV exposure, but because every time I touched him, I could only think about his impending death. Sadness often overwhelmed me because I knew I couldn't change the situation or take away his pain. My strategy had always been to protect him, but this time I couldn't. Sometimes, we have to face our deepest fears alone. I would often look at Ron and wonder how he was processing the news.

A few years after his diagnosis, we went with my family to Montreal's Saint Joseph's Oratory. There is a shrine where Brother André is credited with performing many miracles. In this place of pilgrimage, there is a beautiful section containing hundreds of crutches left behind by those miraculously cured of their ills, and a room filled with candles that visitors can light for special prayer requests. Ron and I did not believe in miracles, but we were moved to light a candle. As Ron lit his candle, I knew that we shared the same prayer: that he would survive his HIV infection. It was very moving to watch him make his prayer request in such a room, all the while knowing what was in his mind and heart. As I watched him, I could feel my heart breaking. Linda, one of the only people who knew Ron's status, later confided that she had asked him what his prayer request was. Ron had replied, "To live."

My relationship with Ron faced challenges on every front, but I knew I would never abandon him. I desperately wanted to avoid the future pain of losing him to AIDS, but the pain of letting him deal with this without me was much greater. I was afraid, but I would never have forgiven myself if I had left him alone because I was unable to face what was coming. I often think that it must be easier to be the one with the terminal illness than the one that must watch their loved one waste away.

But Ron was not dead yet, and during our visit to the shrine in Montreal, there was no visible indication that he was even sick. In fact he wasn't. He had HIV, but it hadn't yet progressed into AIDS. There was a bullet in the chamber, but the gun had not been fired. For quite a long time, we were able to live our lives as though nothing was wrong.

The heavy burden of our secret diminished our ability to be fully present with those we loved. Ron and I had finally wrapped our minds around his diagnosis, but we still chose to delay telling his family. We told ourselves that we were protecting them by not ruining their lives with the news, but really, we were just too scared to tell them. In retrospect, it would have been better to share his diagnosis earlier because we awoke each morning feeling anxious and tense. If we'd had the courage to discuss it with them earlier, we could have avoided four years of daily trepidation. I've since concluded that the fear of what lies ahead is often more painful than the actual concern.

While we waited for the inevitable, my business took a turn for the worse. A bad lease and an unsuccessful attempt at another nightclub led to the loss of the business, our home, our cars, and our savings. When it rains, it pours. Soon, Ron and I found ourselves penniless, unemployed, and living with his parents. It was a humbling experience because until then, everything I'd ever done had been motivated by a desire to be proud and happy, but there I was in my thirties, gay, broke, and living with his HIV-infected partner in his parents' spare bedroom. My life had become a cliché of the worst kind, and it was only going to get worse.

The stress of our financial troubles added to the weight loss Ron suffered from his infection. Family and friends commented on his physical transformation, and although some surely suspected what was going on, no one asked any questions. Perhaps they were too polite or too afraid. Before long, there was no way to keep Ron's diagnosis a secret, so we decided to tell his parents. We had to take some of the weight off our shoulders, but it was depressing to realize that we'd merely be transferring it to theirs.

We scheduled a time with his parents and sat down with them in their small downstairs lounge. Just like at the doctor's office, the experience was surreal. When Ron finally said the words aloud, it was as though someone hit his father with a hammer. Pain consumed his face as he struggled to maintain his composure. His mom managed to keep her cool, at least outwardly, which I'm beginning to think is a skill all mothers possess.

The genie was out of the bottle, and it wasn't pretty. We told them the whole story and they were disappointed that we had kept this burden hidden for so long. We discussed what we knew about HIV and relayed all the information that the doctors had given us. As difficult as the conversation was, I felt lighter when we were finished.

His parents were strong in their faith and were incredibly loving, generous people. The fact that they brought us into their home and fed us for over a year is a testament to that. They were also quiet and reserved, so when the evening was over and our talk was completed, I really couldn't imagine what they'd say to each other when they were alone. Ron was their son and we had just told them that he was battling a terminal disease. Such devastating information can't be quickly absorbed. The worst was yet to come for Ron – I knew it and his parents must have known it, too. They remained so calm, perhaps because they understood that there is no reason to worry about the end when there are so many obstacles to be crossed first. His parents can't have liked Ron's HIV diagnosis any more than I did, but we had no choice but to accept it. Early on, I decided to take baby steps to cope with the gravity of his situation, and although the thought of his eventual death often entered my mind, I refused to let it stay there long.

Plus, I had hope. Ron was still alive. We had time before the end of the world arrived. I had been wrong about so many things along the way, and I prayed that I would be wrong about this, too.

SIX

Accepting What Is

"It is through much tribulation that we enter the kingdom of Heaven."

—THE APOSTLE PAUL

Most of us would prefer to enter the kingdom of Heaven without too much tribulation or pain. When I was younger, I use to wonder why it could not be simpler. I have now come to believe that it is not simple because we are resistant in accepting our true nature as one with God. Even though this world is filled with attack, judgment, illness and death, there is a part of us that wants to be here.

There are certainly moments in which life is easy and peaceful, but they don't last and they surely don't give us the peace of God. Too often, we want to create Heaven here on earth and to achieve this end, we struggle to make the world and the people in it be what we need them to be so we can feel happy, safe, and loved. This struggle is how tribulation enters the picture, for when our efforts to achieve lasting happiness don't work (which is always), we experience pain and fear. This pain ultimately motivates us to question our methods. Willingness to question begins our journey back the kingdom of Heaven.

It is worth remembering that the journey to Heaven requires *much* tribulation. It won't just be a few difficulties that lead us to Heaven's door, it will be many. Our resistance to knowing our true self is too great, and therefore, much tribulation is required to soften us into questioning and looking within. Like a steak that must be pounded before it becomes tender, we too can take a beating. Our growth will be experienced as a process that will comprise tears, sadness, and disappointment, but if we pay attention to life's signposts, we will notice how one part of our life seeks to branch out into spiritual awareness while another continues to address life's challenges.

This was true for me while Ron fought his illness, although my desire to grow spiritually was minimal. I had been so absorbed in trying to find ways to protect Ron that everything around me took second place, including my spirituality. Ron's HIV status wasn't enough tribulation to encourage me to look within, so the universe decided to give me a little more. In 1992, an unsympathetic doctor broke the news that I was HIV positive, too. As steaks go, I guess I'm a pretty tough one. The news was not a complete surprise. The large, horrendously painful canker sores in my mouth had given me a clue that something was wrong. I shared my news with the people who I felt could handle it, including a few members of my family, Ron, and his family. My life as a gay man had become a pure cliché, and although my new health status numbed me, I had no time to lick my wounds or reflect on my situation. Ron's health had taken a turn for the worse and he was rapidly losing weight.

Somewhere along the way, he contracted cryptosporidium, a gastrointestinal illness that causes constant diarrhea. In less than a month, he had dropped from 150 pounds to 110 pounds, and what had once been a very attractive young man became nothing more than a walking skeleton. It was difficult to endure the glances of passersby on the street because in the past, they would notice Ron's striking good looks, but now their faces showed sadness, bewilderment, and even fear.

As Ron continued to lose weight, we considered canceling a planned trip to Florida with family and friends. We consulted Ron's doctor, who suggested that we take our trip as planned since the sun would do him some good. The trip almost killed him. We later discovered that the doctor we'd selected to address Ron's cryptosporidium was completely inept and apparently unaware of how to effectively address issues related to HIV. Ron's severe weight loss gave us a sense of urgency, so we hadn't properly vetted this doctor's reputation. We followed his advice and took our trip as scheduled.

Ron tried to keep up with us in Florida, but he was at his rope's end. He had absolutely no strength left and I couldn't wait to return home. As we flew back to New York, Ron was so sick that I actually considered creating a scene to divert the airplane.

Ron has his flaws, as we all do, but he is one of the strongest, bravest people I know. Nothing and no one scared him. He was sad about his situation, but he mostly felt badly for his family and what they had to endure. He was not afraid of what was coming. He tried to comfort and reassure me, but I was inconsolable. The fire of panic in my heart could not be put out.

When the plane landed at LaGuardia, Ron and I went home to our apartment in Battery Park City in downtown

Manhattan. The next day, Ron was admitted into New York City's dismal downtown hospital. He shared a room with an elderly Alzheimer's patient who incessantly searched for his glasses, while criminal patients in handcuffs walked the halls with police escorts. It was a depressing place to be even if one was only a visitor.

Ironically, we found a lifeline at this depressing hospital. A kind nurse recognized our pain and strife, and pulled Linda aside to tell her that Ron's doctor was a well-known quack. She discreetly gave us the name of a better doctor, and we immediately called for an appointment. That nurse was our angel, and I was moved by the notion that angels appear in our darkest hour.

Without delay, I checked Ron out of that hospital, and the next day, we met with the new doctor. His mother joined us for the appointment, eager to meet a competent doctor. Unlike so many previous appointments, I was able to stay connected and did not feel like I was in a bad dream. After fighting Ron's HIV for so many years and then battling it myself, I was able to face almost any situation head-on. Ron was too weak to even speak, so his mother and I detailed his medical history. The doctor didn't say much; he just listened intently. It was obvious that he had seen and heard this all before. When we were finished, the doctor performed a brief examination on Ron. Ron's situation was so grave that he insisted we check him into St. Vincent's Hospital *immediately*, but Ron was stubborn and demanded that we wait until the next day. Unless he fell unconscious in front of us, there was no point in arguing with him, so we did it his way.

That night, his mom slept in the living room and I attempted to rest next to Ron in our bed. He didn't have the strength to get up and he could no longer control his bowel movements, so I put down a sheet of plastic to make it easier to clean the dark, oily diarrhea that spilled out of him. As I tried to rest during that long night, the large canker sores in my mouth ached tremendously. I stared out the window at the majestic World Trade Center towers and understood that this was my lot in life. How typical it would be, I thought, for two gay lovers to die of AIDS. It bothered me that some people would relish such a thing and think it deserved and I wondered how many would cry for our loss. Accepting that this was going to be the way my life would end, part of me just wanted it to be over. because I began to think that actual death was likely less traumatic than the anticipation of it.

The next morning, we hailed a cab to take the three of us to the hospital and asked the cab driver to take us to St. Vincent's Hospital. He saw our worried faces and Ron's bony frame, and asked me what was wrong. I realize now that he wasn't being nosey, but was actually concerned in a very empathic way. Alas, my stress got the better of me and I indignantly told him that it was not his concern.

He dropped us off at the emergency entrance and refused to take any money for the fare. Imagine such generosity from a New York City taxi driver! I immediately felt guilty for my short temper, but had no time to dwell on it because it seemed like Ron was dying. I will never forget that cab driver who saw our pain and did what he could to ease it.

Ron stayed in the hospital for about three weeks. Intensive fluid replacement and a course of antibiotics stabilized him, and before long, he wanted out. Did I mention that he was stubborn? The nurses trained me on how to administer intravenous drips and since we believed that the home environment could be healing, the doctor reluctantly agreed to release Ron from the hospital. Before we left, his doctor prophetically warned us that the worst was yet to come.

We traveled to his parent's home in Connecticut, hoping that Ron would have the best chance to recuperate with his mother and me working together. Yet, within a week of our arrival, his diarrhea was back with a vengeance and Ron was sicker than ever before. Once, when I stepped outside to gather my thoughts, I found Ron's older sister holding his younger sister as they both cried. Like everyone else, they didn't want to show Ron how afraid they were. I went back inside and discussed the next step with a semiconscious Ron and his parents. We decided that his condition warranted a call to his doctor in New York, and that we needed to bring him back to St. Vincent's that very night. Our friend Lee drove all the way in from New Jersey to pick us up and bring us back to the hospital. Short of an ambulance with a stretcher, her car was the only one comfortable enough for Ron's fragile, bony skeleton to ride in for a long trip. The ride from Connecticut to New York City seemed to take forever, and Ron's discomfort was reminiscent of the plane trip back from Florida. By the time we reached the hospital, Ron no longer had the strength to walk, so I carried his frail, ninety-pound body. As I walked down the street with Ron in my arms, the people we passed were a blur. I entered the emergency room and laid him on a stretcher. A nurse rubbed Ron's forehead, peered into his sunken eyes, and commented on how handsome he was. Ron mustered the strength to quietly say, "I used to be." Tears erupted from my eyes like an explosion, for I could no longer hold them back. As they wheeled him into intensive care, Ron mouthed to me that it would be all right. I'm not sure how long I cried that night.

The next morning, Ron's mom and a friend met me at the hospital and we waited together for an update on his condition. Finally, the doctor informed us that Ron's kidneys were failing.

His mom and I collapsed into each other and cried; it seemed that crying was becoming easier to do. We felt so helpless because all we could do was wait to see how his fate would unfold. I fully believed that death wasn't far away. His mom and I quietly sat in the waiting area for a long while, both praying in our own ways. Eventually, the doctor returned and asked for permission to administer a new HIV drug called a protease inhibitor. Within two days, Ron woke up and said that he felt different. The protease inhibitors had diminished the level of HIV in Ron's blood so that his own immune system could fight the cryptosporidium. Only a few short days before, I was certain that Ron would die, yet here he was, headed toward recovery. For the first time in my life, I felt grateful to be wrong.

It took a full year for Ron's health to improve. During his recovery, he had an incredible amount of gas and would fart almost uncontrollably – a sign of his digestive system healing. It was nice to have something to laugh about again. When you go through something truly harrowing, your priorities shift. Things that previously bothered or embarrassed you no longer have any effect. The prospect of losing someone you love has a way of reprioritizing things. I was actually happy to hear such a noise coming from Ron and was just grateful that he was on the mend.

Eventually, our relationship returned to what it had previously been. Things weren't perfect, but we loved each other. We often spoke about what we had just survived, and some of it was hard for Ron to remember. The experience was seared deeply into my mind, however, and I knew that it had changed me in a profound way. I found myself treating the people at work with more compassion. The issues there couldn't compare to my experience with Ron, and the trite problems that often upset me no longer made waves. I had finally been tenderized. Trauma keeps us centered and can remind us that life is short. The only thing that really matters is to love each other unconditionally, without parameters and without judgment.

It can be easy to keep our ego jacket buttoned tightly, preventing us from being gentle and kind with others, but we don't have to live this way. We can allow life's challenges to undo our buttons and soften our hearts. I have witnessed this transformation in myself and others. Ron wasn't the only patient in the AIDS ward at St. Vincent's Hospital; we experienced a level of gentleness on that floor that can be hard to find on the street. Many of those families, including the numerous caregivers, had become tender and open to love, which I can only attribute to the pain and sadness of being in an environment where fear permeates everything. In such a place, the only real solution is to let love work and to simply be present with what is happening around us.

In the 1982 movie *Gandhi*, the spiritual leader Mahatma Gandhi sat atop a moving train while a battle raged on around him. Despite his awareness of the turmoil, he remained centered and calm, almost as though he was oblivious to it. In a way, that scene reminds me that when we let love in, a quietness falls upon us regardless of external circumstances.

My relationship and experiences with Ron were often filled with tribulation, but they helped to unbutton some of my ego's defenses, leaving me feeling as naked as a newborn baby. My thirteen years with him helped me to reset my priorities and rethink how I want to live. I was reborn. It was an opportunity to start over, a chance to view the world with fresh eyes and without preconceived ideas or judgments of how others should be. Getting in touch with our gentle nature means only that we become willing to view the world as a baby would – without judgment. The tribulations I experienced with Ron were definitely painful, but they brought me to a new level of awareness, and for that, I am grateful.

SEVEN

Relationships May Change, But They Never End

"When we are no longer able to change a situation, we are challenged to change ourselves."

—VIKTOR FRANKL

In this world, there are some things we can change and some things we can't. We can't change who our parents are, but we can change our job, our friends, even our gender. We make thousands of decisions each day, some as small as the decision to go to the grocery store or to join a gym, and some as important as the decision to have a child. The world is a fluid place, and making choices is the only way we achieve change. However, we are sometimes paralyzed into inaction by the fear that a wrong decision could result in despair and unhappiness. If we only understood that we will grow spiritually regardless of the decisions we make, making changes would be less daunting.

I deeply wanted to change the fact that Ron was sick, but I could not. He was sick and I had no power to change that. The only choice I had was to change myself, but the thought never occurred to me. I was so distracted by fear that changing myself never crossed my ego-driven mind. If I had worked on myself instead of trying to will Ron to be healthy, I would have learned how to *be* with his illness instead of having the need to change it. Even so, while it didn't appear that I was making the conscious decision to change myself, I was changing nonetheless.

Like a computer upgrading software in the background, the fear and pain of dealing with Ron's illness resulted in an unconscious willingness to let my spiritual mind guide me, instead of being driven by my ego. This spiritual "background upgrade" resulted in a tenderized version of me, and it was only during Ron's recovery that I began to notice this evolution in my spiritual character, Slowly, I was able to acknowledge that the experience with Ron had unexpectedly set me on course to a different me.

This change did not mean that I had suddenly become a holy man. Rather, I was simply beginning to approach life with a little less ego and a bit more love. My inner change influenced how I interacted with others. I had once been afraid to be honest, but gradually, I began to speak my mind. I learned how to be quiet, when once I couldn't shut up. It became natural to behave this way with each person I encountered because I recognized that everyone deserved my tenderness, not just some. I found it remarkable that this new, gentler me also resulted in the redefining of my relationship with Ron. I don't use the expression "break-up," because as I begin to describe how our relationship changed, I never once felt that the underlining love we shared had become broken.

Almost from the beginning, I worked hard for my relationship with Ron to mirror *The Donna Reed Show.* Everything had to be perfect and idyllic, from our home to our clothes. I now recognize that this was just a façade, an attempt to hide the side of our relationship that was in turmoil. It is still difficult to admit that during my first nine years with Ron, there was little *real* love shared between us. For the most part, we exploited our relationship to satisfy our egos' needs while foolishly pretending it was love. Only during the height of his illness did our ego-centered relationship begin to shift. The imminence of death began to erode the trivial arguments and priorities that we had both taken so seriously. Even as he made a full recovery, the pendulum of unselfish love and clarity of priorities remained with us for a while.

But like the ocean tide, our egos returned to shore. Not long after Ron's recovery, our relationship began to suffer from the same dysfunction that plagued us for so many years. This time, however, I was not so quick to get caught up in my ego's undertow. I had been hopeful that the nightmare of Ron's illness would have propelled us both into spiritual awareness, but it didn't work out that way. I did identify a level of growth within him, but we had traveled to different places.

In the end, I understood that Ron's growth was irrelevant. His spiritual development would be his, and mine would be mine. Comparing the two would incorrectly imply that one's growth is more important than another's. What mattered was that I paid attention to *my* growth, which was substantial enough that even Ron noticed the change.

Eight months after his recovery, we went for our usual walk to Montclair Park in New Jersey to talk and sort out our future. The walk was really an opportunity to discuss our relationship, because we both knew we were approaching a crossroads. This hadn't been the first time we'd had weighty discussions like this, but I'd always remained guarded because I was perpetually trying to avoid an argument. I rarely told the whole truth about what I was thinking and feeling, but this time, I heard myself communicating in ways I had never before dared. I was being gentle with him, yet I had the courage and inner peace to say what I needed to say. Although I could hear myself talking, the words didn't feel like mine. It was as though another person were speaking for me.

The conversation was deep and covered every aspect of our relationship, including my apology for not being stronger in the past. When I finished speaking, a brief silence hung in the air as Ron processed what I'd said. He seemed puzzled to hear such honesty from me, and when he finally spoke, he told me that I had changed, that I had become a different person. He was absolutely right.

Then, he began to express his anger. He was angry that I hadn't had the courage to be myself from the start of our relationship, and he felt that our thirteen years together were not only fraudulent, but a waste of time. In many ways, his anger was justified and I felt guilty. I also wished that I'd had the strength to be less fearful, and although our relationship had perhaps been fraudulent, I never considered it a waste. Regardless of the present state of our relationship, my time with Ron was no doubt the catalyst that inspired change in me. Our individual changes eventually translated into the changing form of our relationship. Like a plant that has grown too big for its pot, Ron and I both knew it was time for new soil.

Two years later, and after many honest, loving conversations, I found myself closing the back door of my rented U-Haul and hugging Ron goodbye. We both cried a little, but even though it was difficult to leave him, I felt blessed that I never had to bury him.

It was the fall of 1999, and as I left New York City with my sister Linda at my side, I gazed up at the magnificent twin towers of the World Trade Center. Little did I know that it would be the last time I would see them standing. Indeed, life is full of changes, and sometimes all we can do is hold on for the ride. I've come to understand that we have no power over what happens to us, but we can control how we interpret it and respond. I could have chosen to view my changing relationship as a bad thing or a good thing, but in fact, it was neither. It just *was*. I learned and grew so much in my years with Ron. The only words that seemed appropriate as I said goodbye were *thank you*.

I found many correlations between my relationship with Ron and the teachings in *The Tao of Pooh* by Benjamin Hoff. Hoff writes about a large boulder that falls into a river, but instead of the river trying to go through the boulder, it simply flows around it. That boulder is a metaphor for all of life's challenges that fall into our path and cause us pain. Our tendency is to become fearful of our unanticipated boulders, but like the river, we can choose to flow around our obstacles instead of fighting them.

It took thirteen years of a complicated relationship and a life-threatening illness for me to accept the challenge to change myself. Boulders continue to fall into my path, but I'm not fighting them, I'm *navigating* them. This is why I could only say "thank you" to Ron upon our parting, because our years together allowed me to see challenges as a natural part of my life's riverbed. It may have appeared that my relationship with Ron was over, but the only thing that really changed was the space between us, not the love. That's what really matters.

As my rented U-Haul rolled through the Adirondack Mountains of upstate New York, I felt an enormous sense of peace. I watched the trees shed their fall foliage and it occurred to me as that so much of my life had not turned out the way I had hoped, wanted, or expected. Yet, as I continued to drive up Interstate 87, I realized that this wasn't necessarily a bad thing.

EIGHT

Bodies May Change, But Who We Are Does Not

"We must no more ask whether the soul and body are one than ask whether the wax and the figure impressed on it are one."

—Aristotle

When I saw my reflection in the mirror as a very young child, I made the mistake we all make: I concluded that I am my reflection. From the world's perspective, it was an accurate conclusion, but when I look in the mirror now, a different reflection attempts to represent me. Instead of a young child, there is a middle-aged man staring back, leading me to wonder what happened to the young boy. What will become of the middle-aged man?

Modern medicine has made it possible for doctors to remove all our limbs, a kidney, and an appendix. They can transplant new hearts, livers, lungs, blood, and bones. When a person undergoes such a procedure, are they no longer themselves? We must consider that our body is not what defines us, and open our minds to the possibility that maybe we are something more.

When I was a child, I had a friend named Susan. She was beautiful and always fashionably dressed, and I loved her sweet smile, her sense of humor, her generosity of spirit, and her kindness. When I worked in New York City, she often stopped by my store to say hello, and when she did, all the guys would ask about her. Today, Susan is a man named Sam. When Susan first told me that she was going to have gender reassignment, I didn't know what to think, partially because I never saw it coming. I knew that she dated women, so I'd always assumed that she was a lesbian. She taught me that it can be a big mistake to make assumptions based on what our eyes see.

My first experience with the transsexual community occurred in 1975, when ophthalmologist and tennis player Richard Raskind became Renée Richards. I was a senior in high school when I saw the story on the evening news, and I remember not understanding why someone would want to do such a thing. If he was a gay man, I thought, why not just stay a gay man? It was hard to wrap my mind around because I still believed that being a man was an integral part of my nature, one that should not and could not be changed. To do so would completely blur one's identity. How could he operate without the specifics of form guiding him?

I've come to understand that the "specifics of form" get us into trouble because they allow us to make judgments about others and provide a roadmap for how others should be treated. From a spiritual perspective, the problem is that *everyone* deserves to be treated with kindness and love, regardless of what they do or look like.

How do you treat or view others of a different religion, gender, physical ability, sexual orientation, political persuasion, or perhaps criminal background? Do you see them as less, better, or equal to you? If you answered anything but "equal," you are giving power to form and this is an ego-driven mistake. The essence of who we are is abstract and is one with our source. Although our eyes may see differences, our minds can choose to recognize each other as the same.

Experiences such as the one I had with Susan, whom I will now refer to as Sam, were instrumental in helping me to recognize that the body is not who we are. If we can learn to accept this, we will be less likely to judge ourselves. For many years, I judged myself harshly for being gay, which was a very difficult mindset to undo. I wondered what it must have been like for Sam. To add a new perspective, I asked Sam if he would write about his struggle with gender identity, and what he has learned about relationships and obtaining peace. Sam writes:

> *I am a transgendered man. I have had the rare experience of being "born" twice: once as an anatomic female, and once as a male. My closest friends threw me an "It's a Boy!" party after my rebirth, which was easily the best birthday party I've ever had.*
>
> *I was first born on December 14, 1962 to a farmhand and his homemaker wife. My father was barely twenty-six years old with a seventh grade education, and my mother was twenty-three with a high school education. My parents believed in the very traditional gender roles born of the 40s and 50s. They were also what I call "Saturday Night Catholics." I'm not sure if there was even a Bible in our house, but every Saturday evening, we went to our town's Catholic Church to hear the same mass we heard every week. Their*

knowledge of the Bible was minimal, yet they believed in God and took everything written in that book as sacred. I was born with a biological defect that no one can see but me, and I was constantly told what God expected of me regardless of how badly 'He' screwed up.

The first time I remember feeling shame was at the age of four. My mother had taken me to get my hair cut, and it was styled rather short. I don't recall having any feelings about it being so short until my father came home that evening. I was playing happily when he came in, looked at me, and yelled very loudly at my mother, "Betty! What to Hell did you do to her hair! She looks like a fuckin' boy!" At that moment, I realized that I was not what I thought I was, and I felt ashamed that I didn't look how I felt I was inside: a boy. I was only interested in playing with "boy" toys. My mother bought me dolls, and I would cry because I wanted a toy truck or a racing car. I wanted to play with toys meant only for boys. Not girls. Ick. But now it was clear – I was not a boy, I was something else. In hindsight, that moment defined a life of conflict, shame, guilt, and an inability to settle into myself.

In my adolescence, there were many nights when I prayed to God to grow me a penis so I could be the boy I knew I was meant to be. I would wake up in the morning and check my drawers to see if he made things right for me, but nothing ever happened. Why did I continue to pray? I was told that if I prayed to God, he would be there for me, but he never seemed to hear my prayers. God never fixed me. I began to think that he was punishing me for something I did in another life.

When I was twelve years old, I had an argument with my mother about wearing a dress. Every time she made me put one on, I felt embarrassed. One day, as we were arguing about my attire, she said, "That's what girls wear!" I screamed back at her, "I don't want to be a fuckin' girl!" It was the first time I verbalized how disgusted I was with my gender. I'm sure she thought I was just being rebellious, but in reality, my repulsion about being born female was genuine.

I spent my high school years and my early twenties trying to accept my gender, while remaining true to my sexual orientation. Since I was about five years old, I knew that I was going to grow up to marry a woman. I had my first girl-crush on my first grade teacher, Mrs. Burk. I told her that one day I would marry her, but she insisted that girls grow up to marry boys. I felt rejected and didn't understand why I had to grow up to be a girl. There wasn't one ounce of girl in me.

My first real relationship with a woman was in high school, and I spent the next eighteen years in "lesbian" relationships, though that term didn't quite seem right. However, I told each of them that I felt trapped in the wrong body before we were intimate. To me, I was their boyfriend, and I was doing the best I could since I had no choice over the body into which I was born.

After fifteen years of trying to live as a lesbian, I finally reached my breaking point in the summer of 1997. I had been dating a woman for two years and I was deeply in love. She was unhappy, and for good reason: like many other FtM (female-to-male) transgendered guys, I never once let any of my partners touch me sexually. I felt such disgust with and dissociation from my genitalia that it was too emotionally painful to let them touch me, so I only touched them. Fed up, my girlfriend left me for my best friend of ten years. That was my breaking point.

After the breakup, I spiraled into a deep depression. I was emotionally numb for the next two years, and finally realized that I could no longer live my life as a lie. A conversation with a friend changed my life forever. I opened up and told her the reason I believed all my relationships had failed miserably: I was living as someone that I wasn't. Her response was kind, loving, and incredibly compassionate. When I left her house that day, something happened to me that I truly can't describe – I let go. In an instant, my mind was changed. I knew what I had to do, and something outside of myself helped me to let go of thirty-five years of shame and guilt. It was gone. For the first time in my entire life, I had true clarity and acceptance of who I was.

As you would expect, my transition to a mind/body gender synergy was painful for my family and enormously difficult for even me to comprehend. But my mind was clear. I didn't feel shame. I feared rejection, but I knew that rejection would have nothing to do with who I was, but about whom they thought I should be.

More than anything, I have learned that so many of our interactions with others are automatically tied to some attachment we have with them. We have experiences with them that we feel are either positive or negative, and then we build our attachments to them based on those experiences. We often automatically define our relationship with them based on those attachments, even on something as basic as their gender. How we go to the bathroom or have sex can drastically change a relationship of many years. My friends and family had formed an attachment to the exterior part of who they thought I was. By modifying my exterior, physical self, I challenged their definition of our relationship. Although I felt that my identity had not changed, they needed to redefine who I was. They needed to let go of their attachments in order to redefine our relationship.

My experiences have taught me that truly being present with those you love requires letting go of your attachments. You must try NOT to give definition to interactions and experiences. Building attachments becomes so automatic that we don't even recognize we're doing it. It has been both a blessing and a curse to have had the experience of my transition. My mind cannot hide from the truth I have learned, but it sure does try to blow smoke up my butt on a regular basis.

Am I more at peace now? No, but not because I regret changing who I am on the outside. I found peace by taking greater responsibility for my life and what goes on in my mind. Before, I made excuses for everything. All my unhappiness was caused by external factors. At least, that was the story I told myself. I told a story and believed that someone else wrote it. Now, I take ownership for my decisions and the path my life takes. It is both liberating and heavy.

Some people may wonder, if I have complete control over what goes on in my mind, why couldn't I choose to accept the body I was born with? My response is simple. I did choose to accept the body I had, which includes my brain. My brain includes the biological makeup for specific gender traits, and in my case, my brain is male. That is part of my biological makeup. I could have chosen to accept this fact and live my life with a male brain and female body, but now we're moving from a question about mindful acceptance to a question about mindful correction. The question now becomes, "Why couldn't you accept your male brain and female body and choose not to correct your body to match your brain?" To my ears, this question sounds as absurd as asking a paraplegic, "Although we can surgically give you the ability to walk again, why can't you accept the fact that you can't walk and choose not to have the surgery?" I would feel uncomfortable asking such a person this question. The discomfort of the question begs yet another question, and you can see how we start to travel down the rabbit hole.

Sam's story is one of courage and change. He transitioned from female to male, but the change he made is no different from changing your hair color, getting a nose job, or losing fifty pounds. There is nothing wrong with changing our physical person if it helps us to feel good and whole, psychologically and emotionally.

The most important change that Sam made was to change his mind. Through the process of changing gender, he was able to understand the problems that arise when we give meaning and attachment to form. Sam has begun to recognize that we are a mind and not a body, and this is a realization we all must make. For most, such recognition is slight, and until we become fully aware of our true nature, we should make changes as needed, be it our hair color or our gender.

Sam and I are still very close. The generosity and character he had as Susan is still there, it is just wrapped differently. We should never disregard anybody or any body, for beyond everyone's shell is a love that says we are not different. This is how we want to connect with others, through our soul, our mind. Our bodies may change, but in this world they serve as a communication device. Things change as a natural part of life. I'm no longer a boy, but a man, and Susan is now Sam, but our minds have not changed.

What really connects us to someone is not their body, but our loving experiences with them. My mother has been gone for several years, but my memories let me travel back to a time when I felt safe, as she and my dad wiped my temple after my fall from bed. Through my memories, I can still experience her in so many ways, even while many would argue that she is no longer here. I had become accustomed to the sound of her voice, her touch, and all the other ways she expressed her love for me, but what matters is not the word or the touch but the love behind them. Love is an experience of peace and acceptance, not judgment. The real relationship I had and will always have with my mother is that experience. Her wax has melted away, but I don't need the wax to feel the warmth of her light.

These metaphors don't take away the grief we feel when we lose someone. Even though I believe that the body is not who we are, I still cry when someone I love is gone. Physicists tell us that light does not die, but is absorbed by another object. Love is like this, and I believe that love is what we are. We cannot die or ever abandon each other. Instead, we flow through each other with an awareness that we are one.

NINE

You're Asking Me If I'm Comfortable?

"Your living is determined not so much by what life brings to you as by the attitude you bring to life; not so much by what happens to you as by the way your mind looks at what happens."

—KHALIL GIBRAN

What life is and what it means to live is an age-old question. Scientifically speaking, if one has a heartbeat but no brain activity, they are considered alive, yet many would argue this is not living. On the other hand, a head of lettuce does not have a heartbeat or brain activity, but it is considered life. The entire discussion of life, reality, and the mind poses an interesting conundrum, yet it is an important discussion to have because how we view the mystery of life and what is real determines the kind of attitude we will have.

Albert Einstein remarked, "Reality is merely an illusion, albeit a very persistent one." *A Course in Miracles* asks, "Can you paint rosy lips upon a skeleton, dress it in loveliness, pet it and pamper it, and make it live?" In the above quote, Khalil Gibran makes a distinction between "you" and "your mind." It is clear to me that Einstein, A *Course in Miracles*, and Khalil Gibran are challenging us to consider the abstract nature of the mind, as well as to reconsider reality and the specifics of the body. You are either a person who hopes to live a measly eighty years only to eventually become part of the earth itself, or you are a mind. You can't be both. If we follow the wisdom of Einstein, A *Course in Miracles*, and Khalil Gibran, the only logical conclusion is that we are a mind. We must consider that perhaps the universe did not make us, but rather, we made it.

We are the authors of the dream, of the universe. This premise can be intellectually appreciated, but is hard to accept because we are so completely embedded in the belief that the body is who we are and that the world is our home. The belief has become true for us. We have gone *out of our minds*, having forgotten our true nature.

There is a way to get back, a way to remember that we are a mind. We must listen to our inner teacher. The loving teacher within us will serve as the conduit back to our minds when we ask for his help. We need his help because the fearful events we endure (as well as the joyful ones) keep our egos stuck. We have a need to solve or maintain them, and these ego distractions prevent us from considering that there is something more to who we are. When this dynamic is examined closely, we see how our lives can either keep us blinded or can be viewed as learning environments to help us recall our true nature.

I don't mean to suggest that we should deny the human experience. There is nothing wrong with experiencing emotional reactions or seeking medical treatment to maintain our bodies. Denying the belief in our humanity is not particularly helpful, so a "compromised approach" to our lives is encouraged. Such an approach will permit us to do what we must as humans, even while we begin to recognize our inherent nature and safety as a mind.

I still cry and laugh, but now I understand *why* I cry and *why* I laugh. Changing my mind about the world is still a process for me, and I have certainly not always done it perfectly, but being imperfect is not a sin and only means that I sometimes need to take small steps in my journey, just as a child does when learning to walk.

By the time I moved away from New York City, I'd had over thirty years of "lessons" before I was finally willing to see things differently. That was just the beginning for me. Although I was inwardly appreciative that I was moving in the right direction, I still felt that I had to conquer my demons.

In October of 1999, I turned forty-three years old. I'd always imagined that I would live to my mid-eighties, so this particular birthday meant that my life was probably halfway over. From my ego's perspective, this observation was depressing. I hadn't accumulated very much money, I had no professional trophies to speak of, and I certainly wasn't the hot ticket that I'd been in my twenties. This observation led me to the conclusion that not only was I going to be poor for the rest of my life, but I'd also be alone. Even if I didn't truly believe that conclusion, I did struggle with depression.

One would think that my experiences with Ron would mean that entering middle age wouldn't have bothered me, but the ego tide has a knack for returning to our shores. My experiences thus far had given me a cosmic kick in the ass, but that kick didn't propel me into total awareness. As I began my new life in upstate New York, I knew it wasn't going to be perfect, but I hoped that my new attitude would give me a chance at happiness.

I moved in with Linda until I could get back on my feet. I took odd jobs here and there until I discovered a new career that suited me: video production. At the time, video technology was quickly changing, and somewhere along the line, the idea of using video to tell my stories came up. I had *no* experience with this kind of work, and now I wonder what I was thinking to even consider pursuing such a profession. Despite the obstacles, I put aside my fear of failure, picked up my credit card, and purchased a camera and editing equipment.

At the risk of bringing childhood traumas to the surface, my first documentary told the story of the remarkable school system that had nearly scared me to death as a kindergartner. The documentary took me nearly four years to produce thanks to my total lack of knowledge of video production, but the project taught me many things about the world of film and left me with experiences that I will forever cherish.

As the project neared completion, I wondered if anyone would like my work. I struggled with ambivalence and anxiety, but then I thought of my former English teacher, reassuring me to have confidence. He had said it so simply that I wondered if he knew something I didn't. His words calmed me a bit, but I still had a flicker of worry that the film would be a flop. I knew it wasn't going to be a Spielberg-level production, but I didn't want to be laughed at, either. I eventually completed *The Pioneer of Rural Schools*, and I was quite proud of the finished product. The documentary was broadcast on a local PBS affiliate, picked up by a distributor in New York City, and eventually led to some national airtime on ABC News.

I felt good about the film, and it was wonderful to feel proud of myself for a change. I knew that my feelings of success were satisfying my ego needs, but I also accepted that as spiritual children, everyone needs a few wins to help us along the way. For me, *The Pioneer of Rural Schools* was a badly needed win. Sometimes, we have to build up our ego before we develop the courage to tear it down.

I'll always remember writing and producing that documentary with fondness, but my memories of that period also include the death of my mother. Interestingly, my childhood fear of her death was more traumatic than her actual passing. By the end, her death was something I was mentally prepared for. Certainly, I shed tears at her funeral and felt a sense of loss at her passing, but it was only a sense. I had already begun to accept that love does not desert us. For my entire life, my mom had been a symbol of unconditional love. She had ego issues, as we all do, but I knew that she would never judge me, no matter what I did. Her love for me never swayed. I'll never be a mother, so it is hard for me to fully appreciate a mother's love for her child, but it brings to mind Elizabeth Stone's comment about motherhood. She said, "Making the decision to have a child – it is momentous. It is to decide forever to have your heart go walking around outside your body."

That's the way my mom made me feel. I was her heart, as all her children were. To a child, this is more important than any toy, and opens the door to happiness wider than money ever could. I have my mother's sense of style, some of her pride, and plenty of her humor. She taught me many things, sometimes without even realizing it. One of those times was near the end of her life. In addition to the mid-level fog of dementia, she suffered from serious leg and back issues that confined her to a wheelchair. Any effort to transfer her out of her wheelchair was always an ordeal for her, accompanied by severe pain. One cold, winter day, I was trying to help her from her wheelchair into the passenger seat of my father's truck. It took five long, painful minutes to get her seated and buckled up. When she was settled, I adjusted her collar and scarf, touched her cheek, and asked her if she was comfortable.

Upon hearing my question, her fog of dementia lifted, and she looked at me with instant clarity and asked, "You're asking *me* if I'm comfortable?" I was astounded. It was surprising to see her brief clarity, but more astonishing still was to see how she saw right through me, despite her dementia. After the ordeal of getting her into the truck, she knew that my question about her comfort was stupid. I had hoped that adjusting her collar and touching her cheek would elicit a *yes* response, thereby alleviating my guilt over her pain and suffering. I couldn't bear to see her in this condition. I wanted her to say, "Yes, I'm comfortable," so that I wouldn't feel so badly. I was being selfish, and she knew it. Instead of honoring her pain, I tried to pretend it wasn't there.

That episode has been a lasting learning experience for me. That day, my mom taught me to be more thoughtful with my questions and comments, and that we can use them to avoid connecting with what we are feeling. In fact, the "You're asking me if I'm comfortable?" question has become a lighthearted comeback for my family and friends. When we recognize that one of us is asking a stupid question to avoid dealing with our guilt, we use this line, even if it doesn't relate to the subject at hand.

Guilt is a suave and menacing thing. If we aren't careful, we will be like an ostrich with our head in the sand, never truly being honest with ourselves about uncomfortable situations. It is too easy to avoid feelings we don't like.

It took me a long time to grasp the concept of guilt. The psychological, spiritual text, *A Course in Miracles*, has given me a theoretical basis of understanding. Nonetheless, it was my mother, a symbol of love, who showed me how guilt can be used by our egos as a way *not to look*. Thanks to her, I now pay attention to everything I say and do.

With *The Pioneer of Rural Schools* project behind me, it was time to move on to the next. I wasn't sure how long I was supposed to rest on my laurels, but I intended to give myself some time to enjoy my achievement before I selected my next project. I was already concerned that my next endeavor wouldn't be as successful as the last, and I didn't even have an idea of what it would be, yet! Fear is persistent, indeed.

TEN

A Book Prompts a Film

"Nothing real can be threatened. Nothing unreal exists. Herein lies the peace of God."

—A COURSE IN MIRACLES

In my early days, I was the type of man who wanted to grasp the philosophical picture of life. To that end, much of my perspective of meaning and purpose has been derived from my real life experiences and *A Course in Miracles*. Unlike the Bible, many readers may never have heard of this book. I have no intention or need to promote *A Course in Miracles*, but I mention it only because it holds personal meaning for me. I hope that my readers appreciate my discomfort with evangelizing, and understand that I have no desire to promote one belief system over another. In fact, *A Course in Miracles* itself reminds us that we should not take another's theology as our own, but neither should we judge it. The book moved me along my personal journey, and I would be remiss if I didn't recognize that it played a part in my personal growth.

My first experience with *A Course in Miracles* came in 1985. I had given traditional Christianity a comprehensive go of it, but the inclination of many Christians to judge others based on their differences left me feeling spiritually hollow. I longed to understand God, but could not seem to get a handle on his nature. I concluded that all I could attribute to God was that he was love. If I was to know more, I figured that it would be revealed to me. When Linda gave me a copy of *A Course in Miracles,* the word *Miracle* in the title and its use of Christian terminology made me very uncomfortable, but I trusted her judgment and decided to give it a look. Initially, I found it difficult to read and understand, but something about it moved me.

Regardless of my subtle attraction to the book, I felt unable to fully grasp its teachings and put it down. When Ron became very sick, I decided to pick it back up, and upon my re-visit, some of the principles seemed less overwhelming to me. This improved clarity motivated me to study its psychological and spiritual meta-physics more deeply, and I soon fell in love with its consistent, rational, logical teachings as well as its declaration that the nature of God is non-dualistic. In other words, there is God and nothing else but God.

To that end, *A Course in Miracles* puts forth a theoretical premise to explain the world we live in. Fundamentally speaking, the book reminds us that our inherent nature is abstract and one with God, and that this cannot change. Nonetheless, there is a part of us that believes we can indeed separate from our shared oneness from God. This belief in separation results in our experiences of guilt and fear, and leads us to identify with our individualized ego self. Consequently, the ego's solution to our guilt and fear is to repress them and hide from God in this world of time and space. Our guilt and fear then seep through and are projected onto everyone and everything around us. Projected guilt can be seen in the judgment of others, anger, jealousy, depression, impatience, and hate.

The world has become an insane place of fragmented individuals who perpetually try to solve problems and find peace. On the surface, this appears to be a hopeless situation because the world will never offer us true peace. The problems we attempt to solve are not what need addressing, because the *only* issue, the *only* problem, is our unconscious belief in separation from God.

As *A Course in Miracles* points out, the memory of who we are is within us, acting as an inner teacher. This memory, known as the Holy Spirit, teaches us forgiveness and helps us change our mind about the world. Hence, through the Holy Spirit's proper perception, we begin to perceive the world and our lives differently. This reinterpretation of the world helps us understand that which frightens us is really a projection of our inner guilt. This understanding helps us comprehend why we are never angry for the reasons we think, which in turn permits us to address the real problem: our *mistaken* belief in separation.

The depth and scale of the book's teachings goes beyond what I can briefly explain here, but since *A Course in Miracles* was instrumental in defining my belief system, I felt that it was important to discuss as a significant event along my spiritual journey. For the reader who wishes to gain a deeper understanding of what this book teaches, I encourage them to visit www.facim.org. Each reader's journey into awareness will be their own, and may not include *A Course in Miracles*. The subtle beauty here is that your yellow brick road may lead in a different direction than mine, but regardless of the path we each choose to follow, we will eventually awaken and return home.

A Course in Miracles was a powerful ingredient in my journey. Yet, had I not come across it, I am confident that my relationships alone would have delivered me from evil. In fact, the book tells us that, "It is only in relationships that salvation can be found." Had I read that quote thirty years ago, it would have meant nothing to me. How could one's salvation be found in a relationship? I had always been taught that salvation rested in Heaven, although I never fully accepted that belief. To get there, I would have to repent for a sin I felt I had never committed, and do good works so that I may be judged worthy enough to enter. Now, such proclamations appear illogical to me. We don't achieve salvation for something that we must do; through our relationships, we learn that salvation is simply something to which we awaken.

Relationships serve as a vehicle to salvation because they provide us with so many opportunities to read life's signposts. Although most of our relationships are with people, we also have relationships with our bodies, our job, our pets, our illnesses, our cars, our political party, and so on. We find our salvation by way of *all* these relationships, and more often than not, we don't realize that we are implicated in the process. I never once thought that being gay, my first adolescent love, the guys at the gym, Ron, or HIV were driving me forward in my journey. They only seemed like problems to solve, not tools to grow.

It wasn't always obvious that my relationships instigated my growth, but now it appears relatively simple. Each of them frustrated me in one way or another, and it was the angst I felt that ultimately resulted in my willingness to ask the Holy Spirit for help. This took time, and my willingness to ask for help can be compared to leading a horse to water that doesn't want to drink – the horse will only drink when he becomes thirsty. I only developed a thirst for help when the pain of my relationships became unbearable, such was the resistance of my ego. Not only did my relationships result in my readiness for help, but they also served as the subject matter for my second film.

Love's Journey, my second major project, explored the nature of love and the inherent complications of human relationships. It included interviews with the Catholic Church, a Montreal sexologist, and psychotherapist Dr. Kenneth Wapnick. Perspectives regarding passion, feelings, and the psychology behind ego neediness were examined and the underlying spiritual component of our relationships was woven in.

In *Love's Journey*, I addressed passion and love. This topic was important to me because my personal experiences taught me that my emotional reaction to the world could easily be misleading. At twenty years old, the passionate feelings I experienced made me believe that I had found love, and I felt that it would last forever. Like so many young relationships, mine fizzled out rather quickly, and I was disappointed that my feelings had deceived me. My first love is a prime example of how feelings should be respected, but not always trusted. *Love's Journey* made it clear that when it comes to passion, we often mistakenly conclude that love has entered our world, when in fact, the emotional high is likely due to our ego needs being met, not love's arrival.

The film called attention to the reason we feel so good when we win a sports game, are promoted at work, or receive a compliment: our ego is being stroked. Because of our deep-rooted guilt, we feel terrible about ourselves and seek success that can counteract this dismal, albeit unconscious belief. The emotion of lovers is likely so passionate because there is no better high than to have someone love us when we don't love ourselves.

I once chose to be with someone whom I knew was not a good match, simply because it felt *so* good to have someone desire me so badly. Why would I put myself in such a difficult relationship unless it was important for me to feel needed, wanted, and loved? This perpetual inner need compels us to seek love, as well as to find experiences that will help us feel whole or promote a sense of self-worth. Logic should tell us that such a formula to "get" love does not work in this way, because if examined closely, the way we pursue love is not very loving. We are like hunters setting traps, and for us, the prey is love. Like any good hunter, we camouflage ourselves, because to show our guns of neediness would ensure that no one would ever approach us. Instead, we set traps made of false kindness and hollow compliments. We make every attempt to be what we think our partner wants us to be, while our goal is to seize the love we believe the other person can provide. This hunting technique often works, and we confine our captured prey in cages made of manipulation, guilt, and wedding vows. Should our prey escape, the world is full of new possibilities to satisfy our never-ending effort to feed our ravenous egos.

I may not have painted a pretty picture of romance, but I want the reader to realize that what I have described doesn't imply that we are bad; it just means we are afraid. *Love's Journey* reveals that it is almost impossible to be involved with anything or anyone without some level of ego involvement. It is important that we are honest about our relationships, pay attention to our ego motivations, and admit that our initial reason to connect with someone was not to join with them in sharing a common purpose, but rather to *get* something. Furthermore, this self-honesty does not mean we should avoid relationships, but that as we observe our ego involvement, we can also begin to recognize that relationships are an environment in which we can grow.

This is a process, of course. When I was a child, I needed my mother's love and I understood nothing of ego involvement. All I knew was that I had a hunger within me that only my mother could nourish. It took years for me to learn how to feed myself. An old saying goes, "If someone is starving you don't teach them how to grow a garden, you feed them first." As a child, I was starving and I needed the gentle, unconditional love from my mother before I could finally learn how to grow my own garden.

As adults, we are still emotional, spiritual children to some extent, and we want to grow peace in our garden. If we can recognize that relationships can serve as fertile soil for inner growth, instead of devices to meet our ego needs, then our approach will fundamentally change.

Our relationships can still be passionate, but this new type of passion will be characterized by its diminished need to "get" something. (I used the word *diminished* because there is little question that we will continue to be emotionally needy. We are human, after all.) Again, it doesn't matter that we do this perfectly, but that we forgive ourselves when we don't. What we really want is peace. Our relationships can be the vehicle to this end, but it is up to us. The journey back to love will often seem difficult and messy, but it's worth every step.

ELEVEN

Peace Comes from Letting Go

"Each one has to find his peace from within. And peace to be real must be unaffected by outside circumstances."

—Mahatma Gandhi

For a good part of my early life, I wanted to feel peace, but was unsure how to obtain it. In college, my philosophy classes taught me that peace is defined by the absence of fear. With this teaching in mind, I developed my personal formula to attain it. My method was to make every attempt to avoid fearful situations, and for the situations I couldn't avoid, I would try to find resolution. Predictably, my recipe for peace didn't work out very well. As good as I was at manipulating and controlling outside circumstances, I was never able to fully avoid or resolve every fearful situation or achieve lasting peace.

I've since come to accept that some struggles are inescapable, and our only choice is to understand how to *be* with them. Understanding how to be with our struggles or how to be "unaffected by them," as Gandhi suggests, is the real question.

Gandhi's use of the word *unaffected* does not mean that we won't have emotional or physical reactions to the world around us; if a loved one dies, we will cry, and if a truck hits us, we will bleed. Peace occurs at the mind level, not the bodily.

When my first love fizzled, I had emotional reactions that I could not control or prevent any more than I could make Ron well when he was sick. My only real choice was to become at peace with the struggles at the mind level, even as I was emotionally experiencing them at the bodily level. What I didn't understand at the time was that peace must first occur at the mind level before it will be reflected at the bodily level.

My initial inability to recognize the process of peace was due to the formula I had in place. It always made sense that if there was a fire, the *first* thing I needed to do was to put it out. It never occurred to me to give myself a moment to ask the Holy Spirit for help. When I realized that there were some blazes I can't extinguish, such as Ron's illness, I understood that peace is obtained by letting go of control, instead of fighting for it.

I once watched a documentary about the 1989 crash landing of an American Airlines passenger jet in Sioux City, Iowa. A surviving flight attendant recounted her story, and described the incredible amount of fear she experienced as the DC-10's wing hit the ground, causing it to cartwheel and break up. She remembers thinking, "I don't want to be doing this." Seconds later, while she was still conscious, the flames crawled down the aisle of the shattered and broken fuselage. She finally admitted to herself, "This is how I will die." As the interview continued, she described how her admission was the inner acceptance of her situation. Upon making it, she described an overwhelming sense of peace that rushed over her. She blacked out and later woke up in a cornfield, still strapped to her seat. When she regained consciousness and steadied herself, she began helping injured passengers.

That story always stuck with me because it illustrates that when we accept outside circumstances, peace will follow. Clearly, the flight attendant could not change her circumstance. Instead, she removed her inner need *to not be* in a crashing jetliner, and only then did peace find her. We don't always have to be in a situation that we can't control to remove our need. It is true that we often surrender to true peace when we realize we have no other choices, but it doesn't have to be that way. We can do this at any moment, simply by looking within and asking for help.

I've learned that it is better to look within than it is to fight. It is impossible to predict what the circumstances will be or when they will occur, but we will all be faced with situations that require us to ask for help. It took me many years of strife culminating with Ron's illness before I finally let go of the reins of control. It took the flight attendant five seconds.

However long it may take, the reassuring news is that regardless of our resistance to ask for help, we *will* let go eventually. *A Course in Miracles* reminds us that, "Tolerance for pain may be high, but it is not without limit. Eventually everyone begins to recognize, however dimly, that there must be a better way."

Pain always stems from our futile attempts to make this world a place where peace can be found, and sadly, many of us have a high tolerance of trying to do just that. I know the pain and effort it took to avoid being judged for being gay, or the prospect of going to a Christianity-preached Hell, or the stigma of HIV. I was glad to finally hit my threshold for pain, for only then did I begin to accept that there must be a better way. It was not a better way of living in the world, but a better way of *perceiving* it.

My dad is now ninety-seven years old, and I suspect that it

won't be long before he dies. I haven't mentioned him much in this book, but he is a very loving man. The fact that my mother chose to spend over fifty years with him speaks for itself. As I visit him in the nursing home, I'm challenged to look at the frail body of this once incredibly powerful man. Unlike my mother, my father's mind is clear – it is his body that is letting him down. As I attempt to perceive him properly, I try to apply everything I have learned. I'm not ashamed to admit that it isn't easy. Nonetheless, I am determined to observe what he's going through with the same lens that I used with Ron's illness, and I certainly won't be asking him if he is comfortable as a way of deflecting my guilt.

My eyes see an old man, but my heart is able to see the spirit that loved and protected me all my life. When his character has left this stage, I will enjoy my walks with him down memory lane, just as I do with my mother. It will be nice to hear him instruct me as a child to be careful of the tractor, or to advise me to drive carefully as an adolescent. My dad's eventual passing will provide me with another opportunity to look at this world differently and I thank him for that. Truth be told, I thank everyone I've ever encountered, for had I not had the experiences I've mentioned and many I haven't revealed, there would be no book and I would likely still be holding the world accountable for my peace.

My writing has never been intended to give someone peace. Rather, my objective has always been to demonstrate how it is obtained. The circumstances in our lives will invariably serve as a classroom, teaching us where real peace resides. Let us not forget that we journey together through this world, and that peace is our responsibility. No one can give it to us and nothing can take it away.

Acknowledgements

Words Of Encouragement

Many thanks to Lucille Pica of Montreal, for encouraging me to get this book done and for her consistently kind words.

Manuscript Editor

Lori Handelman, my editor for her thoughtful insights and professional style. *www.clear.voice.editors.com*

Book Cover Design By:

Venkata Ramarao

Digital Marketing

Special thanks to Alex Ashline, Chief Learning Officer with WebNoggins for his digital marketing concepts and website design. *www.webnoggins.com*

Love's Journey Documentary

For readers interesting in understanding more about Love and human relationships, I invite them to obtain a copy of my film on Amazon.com by doing a search for "Rick Bechard" or visiting, *www.lovesjourney.us*

About the Author

Rick Bechard was born in 1956 in Plattsburgh, NY. In 2000 he established Lucid Productions and produced the documentary, *The Pioneer of Rural Schools,* which recounts the historical influence of the Chazy Central Rural School in the early 20th century.

His interest in spiritual and philosophical musings resulted in his subsequent documentary, *Love's Journey,* which discusses the nature of Love and the inherent complications of human relationships and features the late Dr. Kenneth Wapnick, with *The Institute For Teaching Inner Peace Through A Course In Miracles.*

From *Pain To Peace* is his first book.

Presently, Rick provides workshops throughout the United States and Canada on the human experience as it relates to the principles of A *Course In Miracles*. For those who seek his perspective, Rick also serves as a Life Coach and is currently in the early development stages of his next book and film.

To contact or know more about Rick, please visit his blog at, *www.rickbechard.com.*